Elementary JavaScript

SIDDHARTH DALAL

Programming for Elementary and Middle School Kids

Ages 10 to ∞

Cover design: Siddharth Dalal and Ahan Dalal
Illustrations: Siddharth Dalal

s1dd.com/js

Printed in the United States of America

First Printing: Aug 2019

ISBN-13
978-1-0776825-6-6
978-1-0787085-4-8
979-8-6636524-7-6

ACKNOWLEDGEMENTS & CREDITS

I would like to thank my son for being my guinea pig for experimenting techniques and concepts on him. Fingers crossed that I haven't ruined code for him forever in my quest to write this book.

My wife, Parchayi did more than her fair share of chores while I spent all my weekends over many months writing this book. (I hope she doesn't find out that the primary purpose of this book was to avoid laundry)

My mom, Damini proofread the book with hawk eyes and any errors left are mine. Check out her book on Samkyha Yoga philosophy on Amazon.

The PokémonTCG API created by Andrew Backes made the game in this book possible. CodePip's Flexbox Froggy, which helped me learn Flexbox, provides a fun way of learning things and let me focus this book more on code.

The photo of riffle shuffle in Chapter 19 was taken by my son, Ahan Dalal.

The Pokémon card images are all obtained from the PokémonTCG API.

The card image of the King of Diamonds was obtained from the open source card image repository here: https://github.com/hayeah/playing-cards-assets

CONTENTS

6

INTRODUCTION

I've been teaching my son how to code since he was 8 years old. Over the years as we worked on code projects, I've tried to see what concepts were easy or hard to grasp and what it took to make code easy. This book will cover enough ground for you to start writing code in JavaScript. The biggest problem that most kids, and adults, have with code is not the actual code itself, but how to translate what they want to do into code. After a couple of years of working on code with me, my son was familiar with syntax but still had a hard time translating ideas to code.

So that will be a focus of this book after the basic concepts are covered and we will do some math and make a Pokémon card game by thinking through what is needed to be done, and then translating all that into code.

We will talk about how to keep code clean, organized and easy to read, write and reuse. Once your code is done, we will go through what to do with it after, like how to put it online so anyone can use what you have built. Then, we also look at how to work on code with friends.

ABOUT THE JAVASCRIPT IN THIS BOOK

In this book, we will try to stay as close to object oriented programming concepts as possible. Don't worry if you don't know what that means. You will by the time you're done.

The code in this book will only work in modern browsers like Chrome, Firefox and Edge (the Windows 10 browser) and has been tested in all three. It will not work Internet Explorer - because we will use syntax from modern JavaScript that Internet Explorer does not support. The new features that we will use make JavaScript a powerful and easy language to code in.

CHAPTER 1: ABOUT CODE, JAVASCRIPT AND THIS BOOK

Code is basically a set of instructions that tell the computer exactly what to do. And to give the computer instructions, you need to talk to it in a language it understands. There are many computer languages like C, C++, Java, PHP and JavaScript. This book obviously is about JavaScript ☺.

WHY JAVASCRIPT?

JavaScript is a relatively easy language to get started with. It is the only language with which you can do almost everything. Internet browsers can run JavaScript. Web servers can run JavaScript. You can build an app that runs on your desktop with JavaScript. You can build a phone app with JavaScript. Many of the things you use every day are built in JavaScript like Skype, Spotify, even VS Code, which we will use for writing all our code in. JavaScript is the only language in which you can build any kind of front end (the thing that the user interacts with) and the back end (all the code that does the things the user doesn't see).

Every big company - Google, Apple, Facebook, Microsoft and many more are working to make JavaScript faster and better. So, JavaScript is a good choice to get started with.

ABOUT CODE, PROGRAMMING AND SOFTWARE

Let me tell you a secret. Code is easy. When you start, it will feel extremely difficult but once you know a few basic things, you can essentially do anything. Dr. Google has the answers to most of your questions when you get stuck.

All you need to do yourself is break the problem you're trying to solve into steps. Write the code for each step and whatever you can't write the code for, you're likely to find someone else with the same question and sometimes with an answer.

In this book we will learn how to do many of the basics, how to avoid rewriting the same code again and again and mainly how to start thinking in code. The book explains good practices that will help you avoid many common mistakes.

USING THIS BOOK AND IF YOU GET STUCK

While you are working on the code in this book, I highly recommend that you type all the code out instead of copy pasting it. Only copy and paste it as a last resort if the code you typed did not work. The entire code for this book is also available for you to download and use here:

https://github.com/sgd2z/elementary-javascript

Chapter 24 will tell you more about how to use this code that you get from the Internet properly. Until you get to Chapter 24, you can just browse the code online and look.

Even after copy pasting, sometimes you might get stuck for something silly like a missing comma or a missing bracket. Chapter 19 is all about finding those problems. If you are seriously stuck, peek at Chapter 19. However, I highly recommend you properly indent your code – you will learn about that in Chapter 4. The tools we use will generally underline common problems for you in red already.

Enjoy! I hope that programming is a rewarding experience for you. Software developers work in all kinds of industries including technology and movie companies, in healthcare, finance, car manufacturing – basically everywhere.

Software engineers can also work from anywhere – from home 🏠, in a plane ✈, on a beach 🏖. All we need is a computer 💻 to make cool things happen.

CHAPTER 2: SETUP

If you are not familiar with using a computer and the internet, ask your parents or a sibling or a friend to help you get everything you need in this section. You may not understand many of the things in this section and we will get to many of them later in the book. For now, just follow the instructions and get setup so we can get started.

BROWSER - CHROME

The first thing we need is an Internet browser. Google Chrome is the recommended browser for following the code in this book. All the screenshots and examples will be from Chrome.

If you do not have Google Chrome, you can download it from here: https://www.google.com/chrome/

CODE EDITOR - VS CODE

To write our code, we will use an editor called Visual Studio Code (VS Code). You can download it from here: https://code.visualstudio.com/. When you install VS Code, make sure to select these options:

This is what VS Code looks like when you first start it:

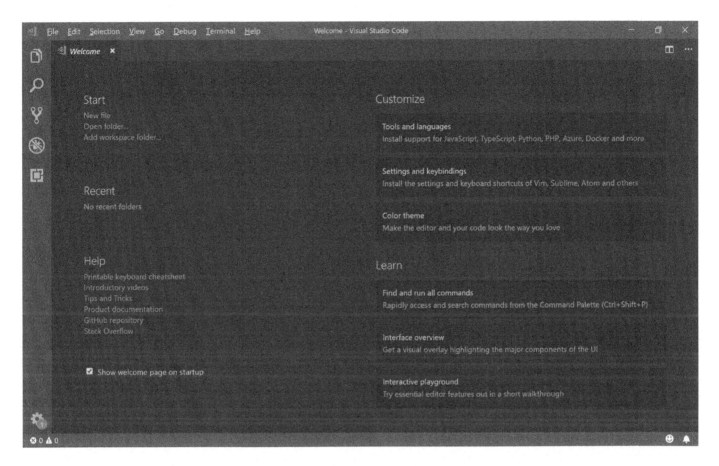

MAKING YOUR FIRST PROJECT

Once you have Chrome and VS Code, here is how we will setup our first project:

Make a folder in Windows Explorer:

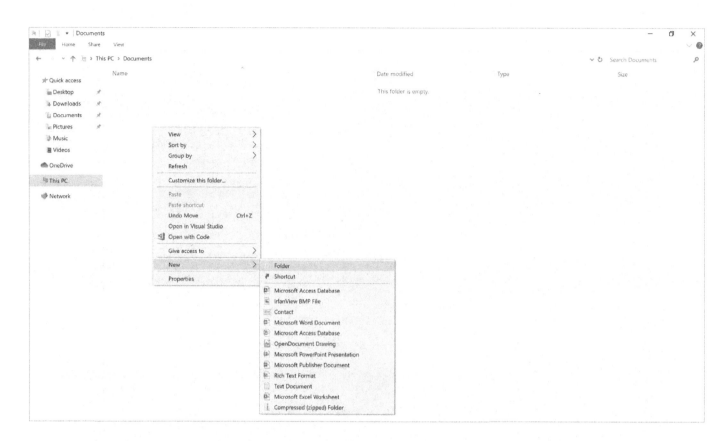

We call our folder "JSProjects". Once you make the folder, right click it and select "Open with Code".

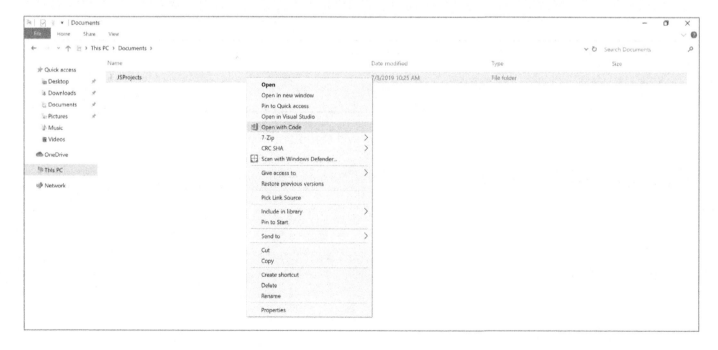

Now this folder will open in VS Code.

THE FIRST JAVASCRIPT FILE

Now let's add our first JavaScript file. In VS Code, right click under the "JSPROJECTS" header and click new file:

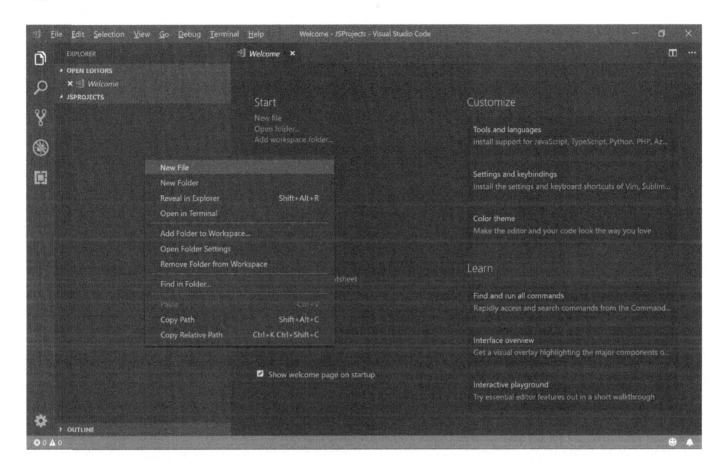

We'll call our file *iAmLearning.js*.

THE HTML FILE

A Browser doesn't directly read a JavaScript file. To make it work, we must make an HTML file and in that we will tell the browser where to find the JavaScript file. Create a new file like we did before, and this time call it *index.html*.

In *index.html*, enter this text below. For now, just follow these instructions. We will talk about HTML later in the book.

14

```html
<html>
    <head></head>
    <body>
        <script src="iAmLearning.js"></script>
    </body>
</html>
```

Hit Ctrl + S to save the file or click on File -> Save in the menu. Now we can get started writing some code.

CHAPTER 3: VARIABLES AND DATA TYPES

L et's get started. The first thing we need to know about code is how to store information in a computer's memory and what kind of information can it store. Along with that we will learn how to do some things with that information, and we will write our first working program!

DATA TYPES

Data Types are the kinds of information a computer understands. These are different for every language. JavaScript understands many data types. The first one is *"Number"*.

As the name suggests, a Number data type is used for numbers. So, if you write

```
5
```

JavaScript will understand that as the number 5. It can also understand numbers with decimals like

```
7.3
```

Another basic type JavaScript understands is *"String"*. Strings basically contain text. To tell JavaScript that you are giving it a String, you put in quotes. Either single or double quotes work. I prefer single quotes in JavaScript, so I'll use them as far as possible in the book. Here is an example of a String:

```
'poop'
```

One more data type JavaScript understands is called *"Boolean"*. That just means a variable that can store true or false. So true and false are special words in JavaScript.

The data types we have talked about so far are called *primitive* data types. As we learn more, we will talk about other data types.

OPERATIONS

The next thing we need to do is tell the computer to do something with the data. Let's take numbers. You can add, subtract, multiply, divide and more using JavaScript. All of this is valid in JavaScript:

```
5 + 4.3
8.5 - 5.5
17 * 5
45 / 3.2
```

You can also join strings together:

```
'poop' + 'stinks'
```

JavaScript will turn that into:

```
'poopstinks'
```

But, what if we do

```
'Poop' + 10
```

In some languages, the computer will complain that you cannot do this. But JavaScript will convert the number into a string and that will result in

```
'Poop10'
```

You can compare if things are equal using the "===" operator

So, `5 === 5` will be `true` (remember what data type `true` is?)

`'a' === 'b'` will be false.

What about `'a' === 'A'`? To the computer, those are two different things. So that will be `false` too.

Often when you see code online, you will see people use the == operator instead of the === operator. The == operator checks if things are equal if you converted them. I highly recommend never using ==.

For example, if you did:

`5 === '5'`, this would be `false`

`5 == '5'`, this would be `true`!

Similarly, to check if things are not equal you use the "!==" operator. There is also a similar "!=" operator for kind of not equal to. To check if things are greater of less than other things, we use the > (greater than) and the < (less than) operators.

`5 !== 10`, this would be `true`

`5 !== '5'`, this would be `true`

`5 != '5'`, this would be `false`

`5 > 5`, this would be `false`

`5 < 5`, this would be `false`

`5 < 50`, this would be `true`

We will use these comparisons in the future often.

OUR FIRST PROGRAM

Let's write our first program that will show something on a page! When we want to write something out on our webpage in JavaScript, we can use a "method" called `document.write`. We will discuss more about what "methods" are later in the book. Here is how we use `document.write`:

`document.write(whateverWeWantToWtrite)`

Let's try to write out some things from what we learned before:

```
document.write(5)
document.write(7.3)
document.write('poop')
document.write('Poop' + 10)
document.write(5 + 4.3)
document.write(8.5 - 5.5)
document.write(17 * 5)
document.write(45 / 3.2)
```

Copy all this into the *iAmLearning.js* file.

18

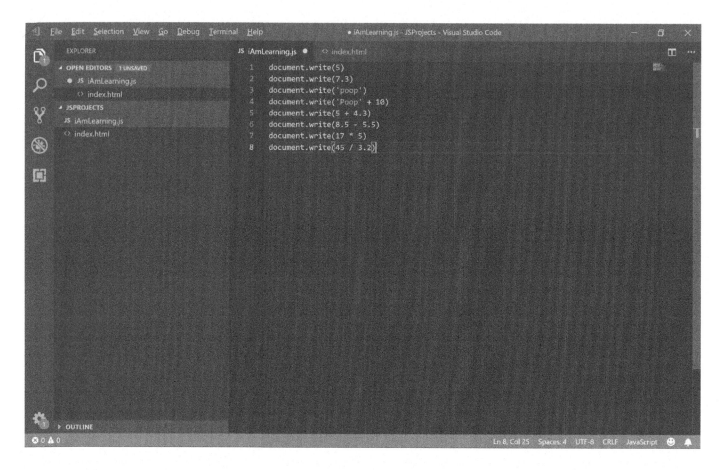

Save the file. Now let's see what our code does. Go back to File Explorer and double click the *index.html* file.

19

It will open Chrome and you will see the results of the code we just wrote:

It put everything all one after another. Well, it is a computer. It follows instructions exactly. We never told it to put things on the next line or put spaces or anything.

Let us see how to do that. The HTML for putting things on the next line is `<br>`. So, to put this on the page, we need to write this after every line:

```
document.write('<br>')
```

Our previous code would become:

```
document.write(5)
document.write('<br>')
document.write(7.3)
document.write('<br>')
document.write('poop')
document.write('<br>')
document.write('Poop' + 10)
document.write('<br>')
document.write(5 + 4.3)
document.write('<br>')
document.write(8.5 - 5.5)
document.write('<br>')
document.write(17 * 5)
document.write('<br>')
document.write(45 / 3.2)
```

Let's see what happens if we save that and reload the page in Chrome:

Hurray! Our first program works!

If you are looking at code online, often you will see people ending lines with semicolons like this:

```
document.write(5);
```

Semicolons are optional in JavaScript and we will not use them in this book

BOXES OF MEMORY

So far so good. We can use the computer to do some math and write some words. The fun hasn't even started yet. Before we can work on something interesting, we need to figure out how to make the computer remember the numbers or data. For that we put things in "variables". Maybe you've heard that word while learning math in school. If not, don't worry.

Think of a computer's memory as a bunch of empty boxes:

Think of a variable as a name we give one of those boxes. Let's say we want to take one of these computer memory boxes and give it a name "geek". Here is how we would do it:

```
let geek
```

The word `let` tells the computer to get an empty box of memory and give it a name. In this case we called the box `geek`. Now, if we wanted to put something in the box, here is how we would do that:

```
let geek = 'Sidd'
```

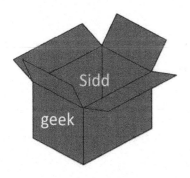

This tells the computer to get an empty box from memory, call it geek and put the value `'Sidd'` in it.

You could do something like:

```
let aNumber = 5
let anotherNumber = 4 * 5
```

This will get more boxes from the computer memory and start putting things in there. In the line – `let anotherNumber = 4 * 5` – the computer will do the math first. So, it will calculate 20. Then it will put that in a box called `anotherNumber`.

Now the fun begins. Whenever you use the name of one of the variables, the computer will go and get the thing you put in that box and use that value instead.

So, if we wrote:

```
let thirdNumber = aNumber + anotherNumber
```

the computer would take the value from `aNumber` and the value from `anotherNumber`, add them up and put the result in a new box called `thirdNumber`.

What if you want to change the value of one of our variables? Then just do this:

```
aNumber = 10
```

Notice how we don't put the `let` keyword. That's because we already have the name or the box. You can't use `let` again with the same name because that name has already been used for a box. You can't get another box and name it the same thing.

What if we want to add 5 to `aNumber` and save it?

```
aNumber + 5 //this won't work, why?
```

This is valid code. But it won't do what we want. This will get the value of `aNumber` and add 5 to it. But it won't put the answer back in the box. To save it back we need to do this:

```
aNumber = aNumber + 5
```

This tells the computer to get the value from `aNumber`, add 5 to it and then put the result back in `aNumber`.

Keep this in mind because we will be doing a lot of this. It might look a little confusing, but if you think about it, it makes sense. To put anything in computer memory, you must always have the variable name to the left of an = sign. Otherwise the computer will not store it. So even if you are trying to change the value of the same variable you need to do something like we did above.

```
aNumber = aNumber + 5
```

```
What happens if you don't put anything in a variable?

let myVariable

In this case the value of myVariable is undefined. undefined is a special data type!
```

Notice how we could change the value of aNumber any time we wanted. While writing very large projects, sometimes we don't want to accidentally change the value of a variable i.e. we don't want someone to put something else in the box again. In those cases, instead of let, we use const to make what we call a constant.

So, a variable can change value, a constant cannot change value.

```
const someNumber = 5

someNumber = 50 // This won't work. There will be an error and your code will stop working
```

It is good code practice to use constants wherever possible. However, to keep the code simple in this book, we'll just use let nearly everywhere.

In this section, you will have noticed the green text that follows two slashes "//". You can put these English statements in your code to help you. They are called comments. The computer doesn't read comments. Those are for us humans who find it easier to read plain English than code. Any time we are writing code, especially something that might be a little complicated, we must put comments in the code.

Later in the book, we will talk more about comments. There are some very special kinds of comments that will help you write better code faster.

```
If you are looking at code online, you will see people create variables using "var":

var geek = 'Sidd';

I highly recommend you use "let". If you see "var" somewhere, just replace it with "let" in your
code.
```

CHAPTER 4: LOOPS - DOING THINGS MANY TIMES

Doing the same thing a thousand times is boring. Not to a computer. You just tell it to go and it will repeat as many times as you tell it and makes no mistakes!

The code to repeat things many times is called a loop. There are many kinds of loops. Trying to teach my son to code, we concluded that the easiest loop to understand is a `while` loop. Therefore, we will only use that as far as possible in this book.

A `while` loop is a loop that keeps repeating the same code 'while' something is `true`. Like this guy keeps running in this circle while he is not tired. When he is tired, he will stop.

Here is a simple way to use a `while` loop to do something 5 times.

```
let counter = 1
while (counter < 6) {
    counter = counter + 1
}
```

Woah! That looks complicated. Relax. It really is not. Let's examine all the pieces of this one at a time:

```
let counter = 1
```

We already know what this does. It assigns the value `1` to a variable called `counter`.

The next line of code sets up our loop:

```
while (counter < 6) {
```

This says that whatever code follows next must be run repeatedly as long as "`counter < 6`" is `true`. "`counter < 6`" is called the *condition* of the loop. We know that the loop keeps on going as long as the *condition* is `true`. So, if `counter` becomes equal to `6` or greater than `6` the code will stop running because now the *condition* is `false`.

What about those curly brackets? Curly brackets mean that the code inside them is a single block. It tells the computer that all that code needs to be executed together. So, when the while loop repeats code, it repeats all the code between the curly brackets.

When we put code in a code block, we indent it. That makes it much easier to read and to tell when code is in a block. Visual Studio Code can automatically indent code for you. Just press "Alt + Shift + F". After you write any code, always press "Alt + Shift + F" so it gets automatically indented. It will help you find simple problems like missing brackets and you will be ☺ instead of ☹ when you are reading your own code.

Now let's look at that same code again:

```
let counter = 1
while (counter < 6) {
    counter = counter + 1
}
```

Inside the loop, each time we take whatever is in counter, add 1 to it and put that new value back in counter. Before our loop starts, counter is 1.

The loop checks if counter is less than 6. It is. It runs the code in the curly brackets once. counter becomes 2.

Then the loop checks if counter is less than 6. It is. So, it runs the code in the brackets a second time. counter becomes 3.

The loop checks if counter is less than 6. It is. It runs the code a 3rd time. counter becomes 4.

The loop checks if counter is less than 6. It is. It runs the code a 4th time. counter becomes 5.

The loop checks if counter is less than 6. It is. It runs the code a 5th time. counter becomes 6.

The loop checks if counter is less than 6. It is not. So, it is done. It doesn't execute the code (just a fancy way of saying run the code) in the curly brackets again. It moves on to the code after that if there is any.

MATH HOMEWORK

Now that we know how to repeat something as many times as we want, let's do something useful. Let's make the computer do some math homework - multiplication tables.

```
let counter = 1
while (counter < 11) {
    document.write(5 * counter)
    document.write('<br>')
    counter = counter + 1
}
```

There. Easy-peasy. The computer just wrote the 5 times tables all the way from 5 to 50.

Now let's look at doing the same thing a little bit differently. We know that multiplication tables are the same thing as skip counting. What if we wanted the computer to skip count by 5 all the way to 50?

```
let counter = 5
while (counter < 51) {
    document.write(counter)
    document.write('<br>')
    counter = counter + 5 //skip count by 5
}
```

Remember, we do need the number 50. If we did `counter < 50` instead of 51, when `counter` became 50, it would stop executing the code in the loop and it would never write the value 50 out.

Instead of `counter < 51` we could use `counter <= 50`. JavaScript has these two operators that we haven't talked about before:

<=: less than or equal to

>=: greater than or equal to

Just for consistency, we will generally stick to using < or > and not <= and >=.

CHAPTER 5: ANOTHER DATA TYPE – LIST (OR ARRAY)

One very important data type inbuilt in JavaScript is the list data type. Lists are called Arrays in computer languages. If you have learned about arrays in math, lists can not only keep lists, they can store multi-dimensional arrays. If you don't know what those are, don't worry. Let's just start with a simple list. You create a list using square brackets:

```
let list = []
```

That code created an empty list.

You can create a list with things in it too:

```
let list = [1, 2, 3, 4, 5]
```

You can add things to a list:

```
list.push(6) // now the list has [1, 2, 3, 4, 5, 6]
```

You can get how long a list is:

```
list.length
```

Before we learn more about lists, we need to learn how computers count. They don't start at 1 like we do. Computers start counting from 0.

Now let's start trying to find something at a specific position in a list. The position of an item in a list is called the *index*. Remember computers start counting at zero. So, the first item in the list is at *index* 0.

If we want to get that item, we do:

```
list[0]
```

For the second item in the list, we do:

```
list[1]
```

What we want to get the last item in our list? That would be

```
list[5]
```

because our list has 6 things in it. The 6th item is at index 5. Remember, we started counting at 0. So, for any list, the last item is at:

```
list[list.length - 1]
```

Now let's put all this together and write it out on the page and we can see what happens:

```
let list = [1, 2, 3, 4, 5]
document.write(list)
document.write('<br>')

list.push(6) // now the list has [1, 2, 3, 4, 5, 6]
document.write(list)
document.write('<br>')

document.write(list.length)
document.write('<br>')

document.write(list[0])
document.write('<br>')

document.write(list[1])
document.write('<br>')

document.write(list[5])
document.write('<br>')

document.write(list[list.length - 1])
```

Here is the result:

Let's talk a little bit about lists and constants. Let's say I made a list like this and tried to use it:

```
const list = [1, 2, 3, 4, 5]
```

```
list.push(6) // This will work
list = [1, 2, 3] // This will not work
```

The second line works even though we are changing the list because we are not putting a new list or a new value in the constant. It is still the same list. The third line doesn't work because you are trying to put something new in the constant. That is, trying to replace what it in the box of memory with something else.

CHAPTER 6: PUTTING LISTS AND LOOPS TOGETHER

Let's get back to our tables loop. What if we don't want to write them out in the loop? What if we want to put them in a list instead? And then we can do something with the list later. This is how to do that:

```
let counter = 5
let tableList = []
while (counter < 51) {
    tableList.push(counter)
    counter = counter + 5
}
document.write(tableList)
```

This is what we get when that code is run:

Was that easy? If not, I recommend reading the code several times and going through it line by line and seeing what is happening. Try to go through the loop like we did in Chapter 4.

MOM'S SHOPPING LIST

Your mom has given you a list of things to buy. You want to show them on the screen one item on each line instead of how we had it above with commas. How would we do that? Here comes something slightly tricky that puts things we have learned so far together:

```
let momsBoringShoppingList = ['eggs', 'milk', 'yogurt', 'things on sale']
let position = 0 //computers start counting at 0
while (position < momsBoringShoppingList.length) {
    let item = momsBoringShoppingList[position] //get the item at position
    document.write(item)
    document.write('<br>')
    position = position + 1
}
```

We started counting at zero. In the loop, it got the item at position 0 and put it in the variable item. Then we wrote the variable.

Then we changed position to 1. We kept going until position was at `momsBoringShoppingList.length`. That is beyond the last item in the list, which if you remember from the when we talked about lists, is at `momsBoringShoppingList.length - 1` so the loop stops.

There is one new thing we learned in this loop. The code in the loop runs many times. Each time it runs we call "`let item = momsBoringShoppingList[position]`". We used the same name for a new box! How is that possible? Remember, we discussed that the code inside curly brackets is called a block? When the code comes to the end of a block, all the variables and constants in that block created using `let` or `const` are deleted. It means those boxes are emptied, the names removed, and they are returned to the computer. So, you can use the same name again.

I think it will help if we read the loop again:

```javascript
let momsBoringShoppingList = ['eggs', 'milk', 'yogurt', 'things on sale']
let position = 0 //computers start counting at 0
while (position < momsBoringShoppingList.length) {
    let item = momsBoringShoppingList[position] //get the item at position
    document.write(item)
    document.write('<br>')
    position = position + 1
}
```

There are many tricky things in it:

- Where do we start?

- What should be the condition for the while loop?

- What should the code in the while loop be?

Keep looking at the code again and again. Soon it will become natural to you too loop through lists.

Here is the same exact thing as the while loop written using different kinds of loops in JavaScript.

You don't need to know any of these to code but as you learn more, you might want to select the right kind of loop for what you are doing to make your code shorter or easier to read:

```
for (let position = 0; position < momsBoringShoppingList.length; position = position + 1) {
    let item = momsBoringShoppingList[position] //get the item at position
    document.write(item)
  document.write('<br>')
}

for (let position in momsBoringShoppingList) {
    let item = momsBoringShoppingList[position] //get the item at position
    document.write(item)
    document.write('<br>')
}

for (let item of momsBoringShoppingList) {
    document.write(item)
    document.write('<br>')
}
```

CHAPTER 7: IF SOMETHING IS TRUE

One of the most basic things to do in code is to check if something is true or false and then based on that do something else. For example, let's say that if a variable aNumber is less than 5, we should add 10 to it:

```
if (aNumber < 5) {
    aNumber = aNumber + 10
}
```

In the above code, the if statement checks if the thing in the round brackets is true. If it is true, it will increase the value of aNumber by 10.

What if we want to add 10 if the variable is less than 5 but we want to add 5 otherwise? Then we use the if statement in combination with an else statement:

```
if (aNumber < 5) {
    aNumber = aNumber + 10
} else {
    aNumber = aNumber + 5
}
```

GOING SHOPPING WITH DAD

Let's try to use the if statement in combination with our momsBoringShoppingList loop above. You and your dad want to save time at the store and split the list into things you buy and the things your dad buys. Let's say this is how you decide to split things:

- If an item has less than 5 characters in the name, you will buy it

- Everything else that has 5 or more characters in the name, your dad will buy

Here is what the code will look like to print out the list of things and who will buy those:

```
let momsBoringShoppingList = ["eggs", "milk", "yogurt", "things on sale"]
let position = 0 //computers start counting at 0
while (position < momsBoringShoppingList.length) {
    let item = momsBoringShoppingList[position] //get the item at position
    if (item.length < 5) {
        document.write('I buy ' + item)
    } else {
        document.write('Dad buys ' + item)
    }
    document.write('<br>')
    position = position + 1
}
```

Let's see what that does:

As usual, if this feels confusing, just read it again. It also helps to delete and rewrite the same code and then see if you can do it without looking.

IFS ANDS AND BUTTS OR IS IT BUTS

What if you want to check if two things are `true` or of one out of many things are `true`. Let's say you wanted to check if `aNumber > 5` and `anotherNumber < 10`. How would you do that? JavaScript allows you to check for multiple conditions using "*logical operators*" like AND and OR. Instead of the words "and" and "or", JavaScript uses && and ||. Here is an example of &&:

```
let aNumber = 6
let anotherNumber = 9
if (aNumber > 5 && anotherNumber < 10) {
    document.write("Yesss!!")
}
```

Let's say your moms shopping list had a few more things and the rules you came up with were:

- If the item has less than 5 characters or the name starts with "b" you will buy it.

- Otherwise your dad will buy it

Here is the code to do that:

```
momsBoringShoppingList = ["eggs",
    "milk",
    "yogurt",
    "things on sale",
    "bread",
    "butter",
    "pizza",
    "corn"
]

while (position < momsBoringShoppingList.length) {
    let item = momsBoringShoppingList[position] //get the item at position
    if (item.length < 5 || item.startsWith("b")) {
        document.write('I buy ' + item)
    } else {
        document.write('Dad buys ' + item)
    }
    document.write('<br>')
    position = position + 1
}
```

Notice the "||" in the code. Now when you run the code it looks like you are getting too many things and your dad not enough. Oh No.

While learning about lists and conditions, we learned a few things about strings! We can get the length of string using string.length and we can check what the string starts with using string.startsWith. Here is the documentation of everything you can with strings - https://developer.mozilla.org/en-US/docs/Web/JavaScript/Reference/Global_Objects/String. Ignore the word "prototype" on the page. For example, the documentation calls startsWith "String.prototype.startsWith()".

```
We can also just check if there is something at all in a variable by checking for undefined.

if (aVariable !== undefined) { // check if there is something in aVariable
```

CHAPTER 8: FUNCTIONS - DON'T REWRITE THE SAME THING

Remember, a few pages ago, I told you that you don't need to write the same code again and again? For that we must put our code in something called a *function*. Then whenever we want to run that code, we just *call* the *function* instead of writing that code again.

Let's say we wanted to write the tables for 5, 7, 9, 14 and 23. Here is what we would need to do based on what we have learned so far:

```
let counter = 1
while (counter < 11) {
    document.write(5 * counter)
    document.write('<br>')
    counter = counter + 1
}

counter = 1
while (counter < 11) {
    document.write(7 * counter)
    document.write('<br>')
    counter = counter + 1
}

counter = 1
while (counter < 11) {
    document.write(9 * counter)
    document.write('<br>')
    counter = counter + 1
}

counter = 1
while (counter < 11) {
    document.write(14 * counter)
```

```
    document.write('<br>')
    counter = counter + 1
}

counter = 1
while (counter < 11) {
    document.write(23 * counter)
    document.write('<br>')
    counter = counter + 1
}
```

That is basically repeating the same while loop again and again. What if we could do something so that we can get the tables for any number we wanted so we don't have to write this same code again and again? That is exactly what we can do using a *function*.

MORE HOMEWORK WITH LESS CODE

Here is how to make a function:

```
const tableMaker = (number) => {
}
```

Remember, I said we will use `let` "nearly" everywhere. For functions we will use constants because we never want someone to overwrite our function accidentally. Using `let` will work just fine but it is not good coding practice. The code above tells the computer that in the constant `tableMaker` it should put a function. This function takes one *parameter* called `number`. And when someone *calls* this function it should run all the code in the curly brackets.

What does all this mean? The best way to understand is with an example:

```
const tableMaker = (number) => {
    let counter = 1
    while (counter < 11) {
        document.write(number * counter)
        document.write('<br>')
        counter = counter + 1
    }
}

tableMaker(5)
```

When we made the function – "const tableMaker = (number) => {" - the (number) in round brackets tells the computer to create a variable called number whenever the function is called. This variable is called a *parameter*.

Look at the last line of the code above – "tableMaker(5)" – this is what it means to call the function. This tells the computer that it should put 5 in the variable number and then run the code in the function. If you instead said – "tableMaker(10)" – it will put the 10 in the variable number and then run the code in the function. So, to get the tables for 5, 7, 9, 14 and 23 like before, this is all we need to do:

```
const tableMaker = (number) => {
    let counter = 1
    while (counter < 11) {
        document.write(number * counter)
        document.write('<br>')
        counter = counter + 1
    }
}

tableMaker(5)
tableMaker(7)
tableMaker(9)
tableMaker(14)
tableMaker(23)
```

See, there is no need to write all the loops over and over again.

You can create functions with many parameters. Let's say, for example, you wanted to have your tables go all the way from number * 1 to number * 20 instead of number * 10?

```
const tableMaker2 = (number, upto) => {
    counter = 1
    while (counter < upto + 1) { // can you figure out why up to + 1??
        document.write(number * counter)
        document.write('<br>')
        counter = counter + 1
    }
}
tableMaker2(5, 10) // 5 times tables up to 5 * 10
tableMaker2(7, 15) // 7 times tables up to 7 * 15
tableMaker2(9, 20) // 9 times tables up to 9 * 20
tableMaker2(14, 10) // 14 times tables up to 14 * 10
tableMaker2(23, 20) // 23 times tables up to 23 * 20
```

There are three different ways to make functions in JavaScript. We have used the newest and best method in this book, and I recommend you always use the method in the book. However, when you look for code online, you might run into the other two methods:

```
function tableMaker(number, upto) {
    counter = 1
    while (counter < upto + 1) {
        document.write(number * counter)
        document.write('<br>')
        counter = counter + 1
    }
}

const tableMaker = function (number, upto) {
    counter = 1
    while (counter < upto + 1) {
        document.write(number * counter)
        document.write('<br>')
        counter = counter + 1
    }
}
```

Exercise

What if we want all the tables from 1 to 10 with each one counting to 20? Combine loops and functions and write that code yourself. Does it work? If not, look in Appendix 1 for a solution.

GETTING RESULTS FROM A FUNCTION

Think of our last `tableMaker` function. It wrote the table on the page. What if we wanted it to put the tables in a list like we did before? How will we get that list out of the function?

Just for that purpose, a function can return a value back when it is done.

```
const tableMaker3 = (number, upto) => {
    counter = 1
    let table = []
    while (counter < upto + 1) {
        table.push[number * counter]
        counter = counter + 1
    }
```

```
    return table
}
```

How do we use the returned value?

```
let fiveTimesTables = tableMaker3(5, 10)
```

This will get the return value from `tableMaker3` and put it in the variable `fiveTimesTables`.

Now let's use everything we know so far to make a function that checks if an item is in a list. It should return `true` if the item exists and `false` if the item doesn't:

```
const numberExistsInList = (number, list) => {
    let position = 0
    while (position < list.length) {
        let item = list[position]
        if (item === number) {
            return true
        }
        position = position + 1
    }
    return false
}
```

Let's examine this code a little more and try to understand how it works. The loop is identical to the one we had before looping through lists. Let's look at the if statement in more detail:

```
        if (item === number) {
            return true
        }
```

This code is in the middle of a loop that is in a function. If a return statement happens in the middle of a loop it not only exits the loop, it also exits the function. Basically, as soon as it finds an item in the list that is equal to number, it returns `true`. If it goes all the way through the loop and it hasn't found anything, it will return `false`.

This is just one way to do things. In code, there are always many ways to do the same thing. Here is another way to do the same thing. See if you understand what is going on:

```
const numberExistsInList = (number, list) => {
    let position = 0
    let found = false
    while (position < list.length) {
        let item = list[position]
```

```
        if (item === number) {
            found = true
            break // this exits the loop immediately
        }
        position = position + 1
    }
    return found
}
```

Here is how we would use this function:

```
let list = [1, 8, 9, 5, 15, 3, 4, 6, 7, 8, 9, 0]
let numberExists1 = numberExistsInList(5, list) // true
let numberExists2 = numberExistsInList(2, list) // false
```

Exercise

Can you write the code to do the following:

- check if a number exists in a list

- If it does not exist in the list, add it to the list

You can use the `numberExistsInList` function to start with. Try it out yourself.

If you get stuck, look at Appendix 2 for an answer.

WHAT IF WE HAVE 100s OF COMPLICATED FUNCTIONS?

Soon we will start on a game and our game will have a lot of code and a lot of functions. When we want to use them, how will we keep track of what those functions do and what parameters to give them? What if the code is very complicated and we need to be able to read what we are doing easily?

Let's try to do something a little more complicated than we have done so far. We'll calculate the LCM (the least common multiple) of two numbers. If you don't know what that is, the LCM of two numbers is the smallest number that is a multiple of both those numbers. For example, if you have two numbers - 6 and 8

- their LCM is 24. There is no smaller number that is a multiple of both those numbers. What do you think is the LCM of 25 and 36? Let's see if we can get the computer to do that for us.

Here is one way to calculate LCM in code:

```
const LCM = (number1, number2) => {
    let start = number1
    while (true) {
        if (start % number2 == 0) {
            return start
        }
        start = start + number1
    }
}
```

Can you understand that code? Probably. But maybe not. There are some new things in there that you have not seen yet like the % operator and `while (true)`. The % operator calculates the remainder of a division. `while (true)` makes a loop that goes on forever. What if the code looked like this instead?

```
/**
 * Calculate the LCM - Least Common Multiple - of two numbers
 * @param {Number} number1
 * @param {Number} number2
 */
const LCM = (number1, number2) => {
    // Start at number1 and keep counting by number1 to get its multiples
    let start = number1
    // This loop goes on forever until we break or return
    while (true) {
        // Check if the number is also divisible by number2
        if (start % number2 == 0) {
            // The first multiple of number1 that is
            // also a multiple of number2
            return start
        }
        // Skip count by number1
        start = start + number1
    }
}
```

All the things in green that start with `//` are just plain English comments about what happens on the next line. You can also put those comments at the end of a line to tell you what happened on that line.

The huge block right before the function that starts with /** and ends with */ is the documentation comment. When you type /** followed by Enter, VS Code automatically makes the whole block for you. All you need to do is enter the description and change the types of your parameters.

This block tells us many things:

```
/**
 * Calculate the LCM - Least Common Multiple - of two numbers
 * @param {Number} number1
 * @param {Number} number2
 */
```

The first line in green tells us what the function does. The next two lines tell us about the parameters to the function. Look at the lines about the parameters. The text in {} is what the data type of the parameter is and then the text in blue is the name of the parameter. You can also write a description of what the parameter is for after the name. We will use this later in the book.

The documentation block helps when you are using the function. As you type code, VS Code will tell you what the parameters are and what types they are and what the function does:

```
LCM(number1: number, number2: number): number

Calculate the LCM - Least Common Multiple - of two numbers

let lcm = LCM(5, 6)
```

So, what was the LCM of 25 and 36?

CHAPTER 9: OBJECTS - REPRESENTING THINGS IN CODE

The last data type we will talk about is objects. Basically things. Objects are how we describe things in JavaScript. You can create objects using curly brackets like this:

```
let boy = {}
```

You can describe objects by giving them "properties". Let's give our boy object a name property and another property that tells us if the boy is a nerd or not. Here is what the code would look like:

```
boy.name = 'Sidd'
boy.nerd = true
```

Just like you can create a list with things in it, you can create an object with properties in it:

```
let boy2 = {
    name: 'Sidd',
    nerd: true
}
```

The properties are also called "keys". You can get a list of the names of all the properties of an object by doing this:

```
let properties = Object.keys(boy)
```

That will give you a list of all the properties of the object boy. So, for our boy object above, `properties` will be: `['name', 'nerd']`

You can use the properties of objects in two different ways. The first is like how we created them:

```
let name = boy.name
```

The second way is with square brackets like a list:

```
let name2 = boy['name']
```

47

The second method is useful when trying to make a loop to list all the properties of an object.

Let's see how to do that.

```
let properties = Object.keys(boy)

let position = 0
while (position < properties.length) {
    let propertyName = properties[position]
    let propertyValue = boy[propertyName]
    position = position + 1
}
```

Look at the code above. We got the properties of the object. Then we made a loop exactly like we did before when we learned about lists and loops to go through the whole list. In the loop here, we do this first – "`let propertyName = properties[position]`" – which gives us the name of the property. Then we do – "`let propertyValue = boy[propertyName]`" – which gives us the value of that property.

The first time the code in the loop executes, `position` will be 0. So, `properties[position]` will be `'name'`. So, `propertyName` will be `'name'`. That will make `boy[propertyName]` the same as saying `boy['name']`.

The second time the code in the loop executes, `position` will be 1. So, `properties[position]` will be `'nerd'`. So `propertyName` will be `'nerd'`. That will make `boy[propertyName]` the same as saying `boy['nerd']`.

We will work with objects a lot more later.

CHAPTER 10: CLASSES - TYPES OF THINGS

In JavaScript, instead of just creating an object with properties, we can define specific kinds of objects. This is the most important aspect of object-oriented programming. Defining types of objects. A specific kind of object is made using something called a `class`. For example, Furniture is a type of an object. And we can have many objects of type furniture. Child is a type of an object. And we can have many children. Or an Animal is a kind of object and we can have many animals.

BOYS AND GIRLS AT PLAY

Let's look at some examples. Here is how we can make a `Child` class:

```
class Child {
}
```

Now if I want to make many children:

```
let ahan = new Child()
let emily = new Child()
let john = new Child()
let rowan = new Child()
```

That is not particularly useful so far. To make this very useful, `classes` provide two different things: *properties* (which we learned about in Objects) and *methods*. *Properties* are things that describe the objects. *Methods* are basically things that the object can do. To make an object do something, we make functions inside the `class`. These special functions are what we call *methods*.

Classes in JavaScript have a special method called `constructor`. Let's make a `class` with the `constructor` method and see how `class` methods are made and what this special method does:

```
class Child {
    constructor(name, nerd) { //This is how you make class methods
        this.name = name
        this.nerd = nerd
    }
}
```

When we create a new object of a `class`, if there is a method called `constructor`, that gets run first and it will get run automatically. We use the `constructor` to set the properties of the object you are creating.

Look at the code above. There are several new things:

- The `class` methods are made a little bit differently than the normal functions that we learned about before. They are made with the name of the method followed by the parameters in round brackets.

- There is a magic word - `this`. We will talk about `this` and see what it does.

Let's see what happens when we create some `Child` objects.

```
let boy1 = new Child('Ahan', true)
let girl1 = new Child('Emily', false)
```

When the first line runs, it will create a variable called `boy1`, it will run the `constructor` method of `class` `Child`. The computer magically knows that it is running the `constructor` for `boy1` and in the `constructor`, we use the magic word `this` to get `boy1`.

When the `constructor` runs the second time for `girl1`, `this` is automatically `girl1`.

So now if we write:

`boy1.name`, it will have `'Ahan'` in it.

`girl1.name` will have `'Emily'` in it.

What do children do? Let's add some things that children do to the `Child` class:

```
class Child {
    constructor(name, nerd) { //This is how you make class methods
        this.name = name
        this.nerd = nerd
    }
```

```
    play(sport) {
        document.write(this.name + ' played ' + sport)
        document.write('<br>')
    }
}
```

The code added a play method to the `Child class`. Let us make the children play something:

```
let boy1 = new Child('Ahan', true)
let girl1 = new Child('Emily', false)
boy1.play("tennis")
girl1.play("soccer")
```

Here is what we get:

Notice how in the `play` method `this.name` magically knew that boy1's name is `'Ahan'` and girl1's name is `'Emily'`. Can you figure out what will happen with this code:

```
let girl2 = new Child('Rowan', true)
girl2.play("with Ahan and Emily")
```

Even before you knew anything about objects, we called a `class` method. In fact, that was one of the first few things that we did in the book! Do you remember what that was? If you guessed `document.write` – you are correct. We called the `write` method of the `document` object. When we are running JavaScript in the browser, there are several built-in objects that the browser creates for us and are available to use. `document` is one of them.

JavaScript itself has many inbuilt objects and `classes` to help you with things. There is an inbuilt Math object to help with math, an inbuilt Date `class` to help with dates and many more. We will learn about some of these later in the book.

Exercise

Can you make an animal `class` yourself? What is your animal like i.e. what properties would your animal `class` have? What can an animal do i.e. what would your `class` methods be? Try it out.

Make some animal objects. Call the methods on them.

There is no wrong answer - well unless your code doesn't work. For an example animal `class` see Appendix 3.

MORE MATH HOMEWORK USING LCM

Remember LCM from Chapter 7? Let's use that to do something useful like some fraction math.

When you are writing code that is complicated, I would recommend that you make your functions and `classes` first but don't put any code in the function of the `class` methods. Put in the documentation comment next. Then inside each function, explain in plain English in comments what you plan to do.

After you have done that try to translate what you have written into code.

Let's try this out and see if it does become easier to write code. We'll write a `class` that does some fraction math:

We can start out by writing out the `class` in a new *fraction.js* file:

```
class Fraction {
    constructor(numerator, denominator) {
        this.numerator = numerator
        this.denominator = denominator
    }

    add(fraction) {
    }
}
```

Now let's add the documentation comments:

```
class Fraction {
    /**
     * A fraction has a numerator and a denominator
     * @param {Number} numerator
     * @param {Number} denominator
     * @example
     * let f1 = new Fraction(2, 3)
     */
```

```
constructor(numerator, denominator) {
    this.numerator = numerator
    this.denominator = denominator
}

/**
 * This adds another fraction to this fraction and returns the result
 * @param {Fraction} fraction
 * @returns Fraction
 *
 * @example
 * let f1 = new Fraction(2, 3)
 * let f2 = new Fraction(3, 4)
 * let f3 = f1.add(f2)
 */
add(fraction) {
}
}
```

We've already done the `constructor`. Let's see what to do in the `add` method. We'll add some comments to it first:

```
/**
 * This adds another fraction to this fraction and returns the result
 * @param {Fraction} fraction
 * @returns Fraction
 *
 * @example
 * let f1 = new Fraction(2, 3)
 * let f2 = new Fraction(3, 4)
 * let f3 = f1.add(f2)
 */
add(fraction) {
    // calculate the LCM of the denominators.

    // Find what the first denominator was multiplied by

    // Multiply the first numerator by that

    // Find what the second denominator was multiplied by

    // Multiply the second numerator by that

    // Add the new numerators
```

```
        // Make the fraction for the answer and return it
    }
```

Once we write out how the logic works - we basically wrote out what is called the algorithm - i.e. the steps to do what we want to do. And once we have that in plain English it makes it much easier to write the code. Can you write the code to add fractions yourself using the comments? You can use the LCM function we wrote before. Try it out. Is the code below similar to what you came up with?

```
/**
 * This adds another fraction to this fraction and returns the result
 * @param {Fraction} fraction
 * @returns Fraction
 *
 * @example
 * let f1 = new Fraction(2, 3)
 * let f2 = new Fraction(3, 4)
 * let f3 = f1.add(f2)
 */
add(fraction) {
    // calculate the LCM of the denominators.
    let lcm = LCM(this.denominator, fraction.denominator)

    // Find what the first denominator was multiplied by
    let firstMultiplier = lcm / this.denominator

    // Multiply the first numerator by that
    let firstNumerator = this.numerator * firstMultiplier

    // Find what the second denominator was multiplied by
    let secondMultiplier = lcm / fraction.denominator

    // Multiply the second numerator by that
    let secondNumerator = fraction.numerator * secondMultiplier

    // Add the new numerators
    let answerNumerator = firstNumerator + secondNumerator

    // Make the fraction for the answer and return it
    let answer = new Fraction(answerNumerator, lcm)
    return answer
}
```

Look how easy it becomes to use our `class` methods!

```
add(fraction: Fraction): void

This adds another fraction to this fraction and returns the result

@returns — Fraction

@example

let f1 = new Fraction(2, 3)
let f2 = new Fraction(3, 4)
let f3 = f1.add(f2)
```
```
let f3 = f1.add()
```

As we try to use our code, it tells us what the method does, what parameters it takes, what types the parameters are, what the function returns and even gives us an example. So now even if we had to use this code after a long time and we've forgotten all about it, we can quickly start using it because we have a lot of useful information.

Let's see if our code works by adding this to the end of *fraction.js*:

```
let f1 = new Fraction(2, 3)
let f2 = new Fraction(3, 4)
let f3 = f1.add(f2)

document.write(f3.numerator + "<br>" + f3.denominator)
```

Let's say you have a friend who is making a cool thing for their teacher and needs fraction code. The friend finds out that you've already done all this work and you give your *fraction.js* file to your friend, that friend can use your code without even reading a single line of code!! Your comments are everything your friend needs. There are even tools that can create documentation files and websites with your comments, and you can give your friend those too!

This is what professional programmers do. They make a documentation site with their code comments and other people using their code just look at the documentation.

We will add this *fraction.js* file to our *index.html* just like we added the *iAmLearning.js* file.

```
<html>
    <head></head>
    <body>
        <script src="iAmLearning.js"></script>
        <script src="fraction.js"></script>
    </body>
</html>
```

Exercise

Make a `subtract` method for the `Fraction` class. See if you can multiply and divide fractions. Maybe this will help you or someone you know to check if your math homework is correct.

THINGS IN OUR POKÉMON GAME

Since we are planning to make a Pokémon card game, let's start thinking of all the objects we will need for the game and what properties and methods they will need. Before we do that, we need to at least have some basic idea about what the game will be. Let's say our game is a two-player game where each player gets some number of Pokémon cards and they attack each other. We'll think of more details later. In real life, when you work on a project, you will have a lot more planning and obviously think of a lot more things before starting. Since we are learning, we will think of what we need as we go along. Here we will get started making some of our `classes`. We will make them work (called implement them) them later.

Pokémon Card

What are the properties of a Pokémon card? Look at the Mega Charizard card and see if you can figure out what properties we would need for our game. Here are some:

- Name

- HP

- Image

- Attacks

The card has many more properties. Can you list some more?

What methods should it have for our game?

- Attack

- Anything else you can think of?

Let's see what our class would look like:

```
class PokemonCard {
    /**
     * A pokemon card must be created with the following properties:
     * @param {String} name
     * @param {Number} HP
     * @param {String} image
     * @param {Array} attacks
     */
    constructor(name, HP, image, attacks) {
        this.name = name
        this.HP = HP
        this.image = image
        this.attacks = attacks
    }

    /**
     * Select one of the attacks and return it
     */
    attack() {

    }
}
```

Player

What are the properties of a Player? Here are some:

- Name

- Cards

- Score

What methods should a player have?

- Play

Let's get started making our player `class`:

```
class Player {
    /**
     * A player has the following properties
     * @param {String} name
     * @param {Array} cards
     */
    constructor(name, cards) {
        this.name = name
        this.cards = cards
        this.score = 0
    }

    /**
     * The player should now take a turn
     */
    play() {

    }
}
```

Notice something different? We didn't pass the score as a parameter to the `constructor`. We just created it in the `constructor` method. You don't need to pass all the properties into the `constructor`. You can create them any time you want in any `class` method.

Game

What about the game itself - what properties should it have?

- Players

What methods should it have?

- Start

- GetPokemonCards

Let's think about some of the things we would need to make our game work.

- We would need to get a list of Pokémon cards from somewhere (we will talk about this in Chapter 20) – maybe this goes in the game constructor?

- We might need to shuffle cards (Chapter 18) – maybe when the game starts? The cards that a player has is a list and we will need to learn how to add and remove things from lists (Chapter 16) – when the game starts and as the players take turns

- We will be writing a lot of code and we need to be able to organize this code (Chapter 15)

- We will need to show more than just text on a page properly (Chapter 11 and 12) – we need to show all the cards on the screen

- We will need to be able to be able to catch actions that the person playing our game makes - like click on cards (Chapter 12)

These are just some of the things we will need to know.

CHAPTER 11: HTML

Now that we have learned so much JavaScript, let's take a short break and look some of the things we can put on a web page. What you see on a web page is written in a language called HTML (HyperText Markup Language). Remember what we put in our *index.html*? Let's have a look at it again:

```
<html>
    <head></head>
    <body>
        <script src="iAmLearning.js"></script>
        <script src="fraction.js"></script>
    </body>
</html>
```

That is basically what HTML looks like. The things between < > are called tags. The page is called a "document", remember document.write? document is a JavaScript object that represents everything that is in between <html> and <html>. The document has two main sections, head and body. Everything you see on the page is what is in the body. There are many different things that you can put in the body of an HTML page. You can put text boxes, drop down boxes, buttons, images and more. In this book we will not be looking at everything in detail. Our focus will be more on how we make some of these things in code. Remember how we used document.write? That was just to get you started showing things on the page.

We are now going to do things like real web developers. The first thing we will do is make containers on the page and put things in these containers. document.write will not work for us going forward, especially after we start splitting our code into files. After we figure out how to put things on a page, we can make things look nice and pretty.

The container we are talking about is called a div. Here is how we make a div in HTML and put some text in it:

```
<div>Hi! I'm some text in a div.</div>
```

Here is how we do the same thing in JavaScript:

```
let myDiv = document.createElement('div') // Create a div
myDiv.innerHTML = "Hi! I'm some text in a div." // Put text in div
document.body.appendChild(myDiv) // put the div on the page
```

Look at the code above. The first line – `let myDiv = document.createElement('div')` – creates a `div`.

The second line – `myDiv.innerHTML = "Hi! I'm some text in a div."` – puts some text in the `div`. Notice that I used double quotes. That's because the text has a single quote in it already. In JavaScript you can use either single quotes or double quotes for a string, remember?

The third line – `document.body.appendChild(myDiv)` – adds the `div` to the body.

Now let's put a text box (a box in which a user can type something) in our `div`. Here is how to do this directly in HTML:

```
<div>Enter Something in this Text Box:
    <input type="text"></input>
</div>
```

Here is how to do it in JavaScript:

```
let myDiv = document.createElement('div')
myDiv.innerHTML = "Enter Something in this Text Box: "
let myTextBox = document.createElement('input') // Create an input element
myTextBox.type = 'text' // Make the input element a text box
myDiv.appendChild(myTextBox) // put the textbox in the div
document.body.appendChild(myDiv)
```

Next, let's put a button next to the text box. Here is how to do this in HTML:

```
<div>Enter Something in this Text Box:
    <input type="text"></input>
    <button>Click Me!</button>
</div>
```

Here is how to do this in JavaScript

```
let myDiv = document.createElement('div')
myDiv.innerHTML = "Enter Something in this Text Box: "
let myTextBox = document.createElement('input')
myTextBox.type = 'text'
myDiv.appendChild(myTextBox)
let myButton = document.createElement('button') // create a button
myButton.innerHTML = 'Click Me!' // put some text on the button
myDiv.appendChild(myButton) // put the button in the div
```

```
document.body.appendChild(myDiv)
```

Things look so much easier and shorter in HTML. Can you think why we would choose to do something in JavaScript or HTML?

One reason to do something in JavaScript is that we don't know in advance how many or what elements are needed on the page. For example, if we were building the Hangman game, we don't know how many letters are in the word in advance before selecting the word. Also, even though we can create all the elements in HTML, we can't really make them do anything much without JavaScript.

Elements that are created in JavaScript are called "dynamically" created elements.

Let's go back to our `PokemonCard` class and see how we can show the card image. Let's add a method to it to show the card image called show. This method will have one parameter – `div` – which will be the `div` that we put the image in. The HTML tag for an image is `'img'`. Can you guess how you create a new image in JavaScript? If you guessed – `document.createElement('img')` – you guessed right.

BACK TO OUR GAME

Let's add a new method to the `PokemonCard` class to show the image in a `div`. To tell the browser where to find the image, the `'img'` element has a property called `src`.

```
class PokemonCard {
    /**
     * A pokemon card must be created with the following properties:
     * @param {String} name
     * @param {Number} HP
     * @param {String} image
     * @param {Array} attacks
     */
```

62

```
    constructor(name, HP, image, attacks) {
        this.name = name
        this.HP = HP
        this.image = image
        this.attacks = attacks
    }


    /**
    * Show the image of this card in the div.
    * @param {HTMLDivElement} div
    */
    show(div) {
        // create the image element
        let image = document.createElement('img')

        // set the src property to this.image
        image.src = this.image

        // put the image element in the div
        div.appendChild(image)
    }
}
```

Here is where you can find an image of the back of a Pokémon card: https://github.com/sgd2z/elementary-javascript/blob/master/Chapter22/images/pokemon_card_back.jpg?raw=true

Let's see if our show code works:

```
// create a new PokemonCard
let charizard = new PokemonCard('charizard', 180, 'https://github.com/sgd2z/elementary-javascript/blob/master/Chapter22/images/pokemon_card_back.jpg?raw=true', {})

// create the div to show the image in
let cardDiv = document.createElement('div')
document.body.appendChild(cardDiv)

// call the show method to put the image in the div
charizard.show(cardDiv)
```

It worked!

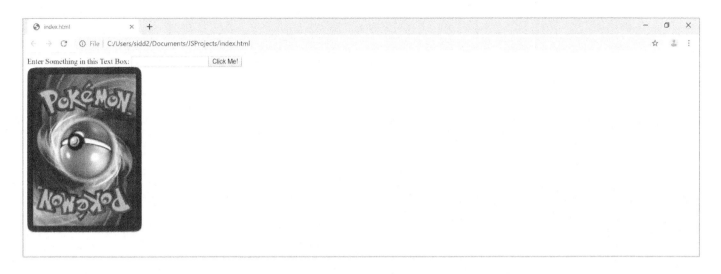

The next thing we will learn will be how to make things happen when the user does something on a page. There are many ways to do this. However, just to keep things consistent and keeping to one way of doing things, we will create all the HTML elements in JavaScript.

CHAPTER 12: EVENTS

W hen a user does something on the page like type text in a text box or click a button, what they are doing is making "events" happen. With JavaScript we can listen for these events and do things.

Some commonly used events are keypress, which happens when the user presses a key on the keyboard and click, which happens when the user clicks a mouse button. Let's see how we can do something when a user clicks a button:

```
let myDiv = document.createElement('div')
myDiv.innerHTML = "Enter Something in this Text Box: "
let myTextBox = document.createElement('input')
myTextBox.type = 'text'
myDiv.appendChild(myTextBox)
let myButton = document.createElement('button')

// create a function that we will call when the button is clicked:
const doSomethingWhenButtonIsClicked = () => {
    alert(myTextBox.value); // show a popup with the text in the textbox
}

// addEventListener is how we listen to when things happen:
myButton.addEventListener('click', doSomethingWhenButtonIsClicked)

myButton.innerHTML = 'Click Me!'
myDiv.appendChild(myButton)
document.body.appendChild(myDiv)
```

Look at the code above. We used a method called addEventListener of an HTML element which lets us call a function when some event happens. addEventListener takes two parameters:

- the name of the event

- the function to call when the event happens

In this case the event is `'click'`, which happens when the user clicks on the element. And the function to call when the user clicks is `doSomethingWhenButtonIsClicked`.

In the code above we also used the `value` property of the text box to get us what the user has typed in it.

Here is what happens when the button is clicked:

Exercise

Remember our tables code from before? With what you know now, can you write the code to write the tables for a number entered in a text box?

* * *

Now that we know how to add a listener for an event, it is important to know how to remove that listener. Here is how to remove a listener:

```
myButton.removeEventListener('click', doSomethingWhenButtonIsClicked)
```

Let's say we only want the user to click a button only one time, how would we remove the listener?

```
const doSomethingWhenButtonIsClicked = () => {
    // remove the listener when the button is clicked.
    myButton.removeEventListener('click', doSomethingWhenButtonIsClicked)
    alert(myTextBox.value); // show a popup with the text in the textbox
}
```

Try clicking the button twice after making this change.

BACK TO OUR GAME

Let's see if we can click on that card image of ours and flip it over when the user clicks on it. When we show the image, we will show the image for the back of the card and add an event listener for click. And when the image is clicked, we will show the image of Charizard. That is how we will "flip" the card – by changing the image that is shown. Here is where to find the image of a Charizard card:

https://images.pokemontcg.io/det1/5_hires.png

Let's see how our code needs to change to make this happen (The constructor and other parts are not shown here):

```
class PokemonCard {
    /**
     * Show the image of this card in the div.
     * @param {HTMLDivElement} div
     */
    show(div) {
        // create the image element
        let image = document.createElement('img')

        // set the src property to the back of the card
        image.src = 'https://github.com/sgd2z/elementary-
javascript/blob/master/Chapter22/images/pokemon_card_back.jpg?raw=true'

        // put the image element in the div
        div.appendChild(image)

        const showImage = () => {
            image.removeEventListener('click', showImage)
            image.src = this.image
        }

        // add click listener
        image.addEventListener('click', showImage)
    }
}

// create a new PokemonCard
let charizard = new PokemonCard('charizard', 180,
'https://images.pokemontcg.io/det1/5_hires.png', {})
```

```
// create the div to show the image in
let cardDiv = document.createElement('div')
document.body.appendChild(cardDiv)

// call the show method to put the image in the div
charizard.show(cardDiv)
```

Test if this worked for you. It did for me! But the Charizard image was much bigger than the back of the card. We'll learn how to fix that in the next chapter.

CHAPTER 13: MAKING THINGS PRETTY: CSS

Now we know enough about doing many things we need with code, let see how to make things look nice. The way to make things colorful and nice on HTML pages is via something called CSS (Cascading Style Sheets). We can change fonts, colors, backgrounds, borders and size and position things properly with CSS.

Let's make a CSS file called *mystyles.css* to put some styles in

Here is how to tell the HTML file how to find the stylesheet:

```
<link rel="stylesheet" href="mystyles.css"></link>
```

This goes in the `<head>` section of the HTML file:

```
<html>
    <head>
        <link rel="stylesheet" href="mystyles.css"></link>
    </head>
    <body>
        <script src="iAmLearning.js"></script>
    </body>
</html>
```

We can apply CSS to specific HTML elements either by what element it is or to a specific element or to a collection of elements.

STYLING ALL ELEMENTS OF A TYPE

Let's say we want to style all `div`s. The way to do that would be to put this in the CSS File

```
div {
}
```

The styles go between the curly brackets. For example, if we want to set the font size:

```
div {
    font-size: 20px;
}
```

Let's say we want to change multiple things - Add a border, change the color of the text and add a background:

```
div {
    font-size: 20px;
    color: red;
    background-color: lightgreen;
    border-color: darkgreen;
    border-width: 1px;
    border-style: solid
}
```

Notice how there are semicolons after every style. Unlike in JavaScript, semicolons are mandatory in CSS on all lines in a style block except the last one.

STYLING AN INDIVIDUAL ELEMENT

To style an individual element, like one specific `div` or one specific input box, we need to give that element an id.

Here is how we give something an id in HTML:

```
<div id="thisIsMyDiv">Hi! I'm some text in a div.</div>
```

Here is how we do it in Javascript:

```
let myDiv = document.createElement('div')
myDiv.id ='thisIsMyDiv'
myDiv.innerHTML = "Hi! I'm some text in a div."
document.body.appendChild(myDiv)
```

Here is how to style something with the id `'thisIsMyDiv'`

```
#thisIsMyDiv {
```

```
    font-size: 15px;
    color: cyan;
    background-color: navy;
    border-color: red;
    border-width: 5px;
    border-style: dashed
}
```

Notice the # in front of the id.

You can also style an element in JavaScript without a CSS file. Here is how we would do that:

```
let myDiv = document.createElement('div')
myDiv.innerHTML = "Hi! I'm some text in a div."
document.body.appendChild(myDiv)
myDiv.style.fontSize = "15px"
myDiv.style.color = "cyan"
myDiv.style.backgroundColor = "navy"
myDiv.style.borderColor = "red"
myDiv.style.borderWidth = "5px"
myDiv.style.borderStyle = "dashed"
```

Notice how the names of the same properties change. In the stylesheet what was called font-size is called fontSize in JavaScript. That's because you cannot use dashes in JavaScript variables or property names. Generally, we won't style things in JavaScript unless necessary because in real life, often styles and code are responsibilities of different people and it is standard practice to keep styles separate from code.

STYLING A GROUP OF ELEMENTS

To style a group of elements, like several divs or several images or even elements of different types, we add them to a "CSS class". Note that a CSS class has nothing to do with the classes we learned about before in JavaScript. These classes are just a way to group HTML elements for styling.

Here is how to add CSS classes to elements in HTML:

```
<div class="bigred">This div has the bigred class</div>
<div class="smallblue">This div has the smallblue class</div>
```

Here is how to add CSS classes to elements in JavaScript

```
let bigRed = document.createElement('div')
```

```
bigRed.classList.add('bigred')
bigRed.innerHTML = 'This div has the bigred class'
document.body.appendChild(bigRed)

let smallBlue = document.createElement('div')
smallBlue.classList.add('smallblue')
smallBlue.innerHTML = 'This div has the smallblue class'
document.body.appendChild(smallBlue)
```

Now let's add these classes to our CSS File

```
.bigred {
    font-size: 25px;
    color: red
}

.smallblue {
    font-size: 10px;
    color: blue
}
```

Notice the . in front of the name of the CSS class.

Here is what this looks like on the page (zoomed for visibility):

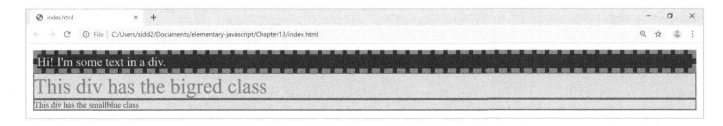

Look at that. So in our three `div`s above, first all the styles for `div` were applied. Then for the `div` with the id `thisIsMyDiv` all the styles specified by `#thisIsMyDiv` were applied in addition to the ones for `div`. Note that this has `font-size` is `15px` and it overwrote the one in `div` for `20px`. Same thing for `color`.

You can even add multiple classes to an element. Let's say we wanted `smallblue`, `bigblue`, `smallred` and `bigred`, `smallpurple` and `bigpurple` we wouldn't have to make six different classes and put a `font-size` and a `color` in each one. We can make separate ones for `color` and separate ones for `font-size` like this:

```
.big {
    font-size: 25px
}
.small {
    font-size: 10px
}
.red {
    color: red
}
.blue {
    color: blue
}
.purple {
    color: purple
}
```

Let's see how we can use these in combination.

Here is how to do this in HTML:

```
<div class="big red">Some Text</div>
<div class="big blue">Some Text</div>
<div class="big purple">Some Text</div>
<div class="small red">Some Text</div>
<div class="small blue">Some Text</div>
<div class="small purple">Some Text</div>
```

Let's see how we will do this in JavaScript. Instead of creating each `div` individually, how about we use some loops:

```javascript
let colorList = ['red', 'blue', 'purple']
let position = 0
while (position < colorList.length) {
    let div = document.createElement('div')
    div.innerHTML = 'Some Text'
    div.classList.add("big", colorList[position])
    document.body.appendChild(div)
    position = position + 1
}

position = 0
while (position < colorList.length) {
    let div = document.createElement('div')
    div.innerHTML = 'Some Text'
    div.classList.add("small", colorList[position])
    document.body.appendChild(div)
    position = position + 1
}
```

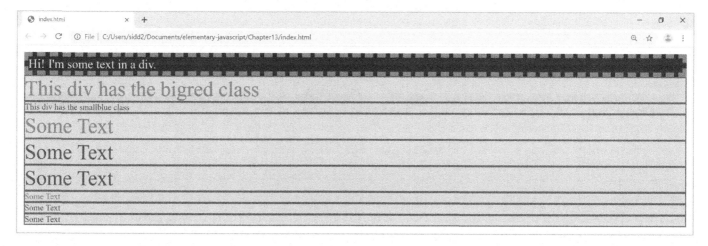

CSS MEASUREMENT UNITS

In all the styles above, we used pixels (px) as the measurement unit for fonts. There are many measurement units available in CSS but for this book we will stick to pixels and percent (%). We will size elements using % where we need to size them. Percent sizing for elements sizes them as a percent of the element they are in.

Let's see what that means by creating a few `div`s:

```
let div1 = document.createElement('div')
let div2 = document.createElement('div')
let div3 = document.createElement('div')
let div4 = document.createElement('div')
div1.classList.add('fiftypercent')
div2.classList.add('fiftypercent')
div3.classList.add('fiftypercent')
div4.classList.add('fiftypercent')
div1.innerHTML = "div1"
div2.innerHTML = "div2"
div3.innerHTML = "div3"
div4.innerHTML = "div4"
document.body.appendChild(div1)
div1.appendChild(div2)
div2.appendChild(div3)
div3.appendChild(div4)
```

Here is the what to put in *styles.css*:

```
.fiftypercent {
    width: 50%
}
```

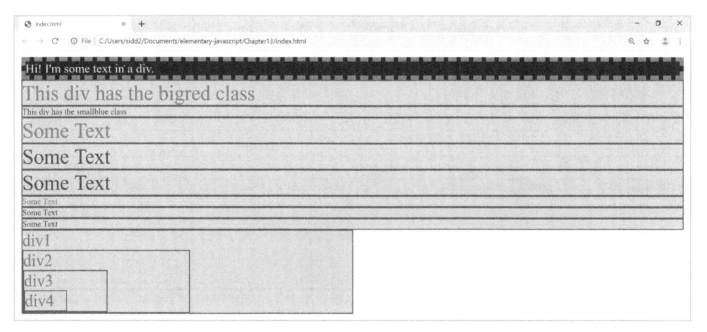

Look at that! `div1` is 50% of the width of the `body`. `div2` is 50% of the width of the `div1`. `div3` Is 50% of the width of `div2`. `div4`is 50% of the width of `div3`.

THE SIZE OF THINGS: CSS BOX MODEL

The image to the left shows you how elements are sized. Having so many different things makes it very confusing to size things in JavaScript and HTML.

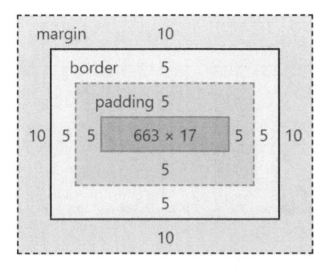

In CSS, the `width` and `height` properties set the width and height of the blue box in the photo, which represents the actual element but do not include `padding`, `border` or `margin`.

`padding` is the gap between the border and the element. `border` is the border around the element. `margin` is the spacing outside the border of the element.

In JavaScript, there are two kinds of width and height:

- `offsetWidth` and `offsetHeight`: these include the element, the `padding` and the `border`, but **not** the `margin`

- `clientWidth` and `clientWidth`: these include the element and the `padding`, but **not** the `border` and the `margin`.

Let's try this out on an element. We will only specify `width`s to see what happens. First, we will create a `div` with no `margin` or `padding`, just a `border` and we will put another `div` in it with `margin`, `padding` and a `border` and see what happens. Here is the CSS:

```css
.outerdiv {
    width: 200px;
    border: 1px;
    border-color: yellowgreen;
    border-style: solid;
    padding: 0px;
    margin: 0px
}

.innerdiv {
    width: 100%;
```

```
    border-width: 20px;
    border-color: navy;
    border-style: solid;
    margin: 20px;
    padding: 20px;
    background-color: cyan
}
```

Here is the JavaScript:

```
let outerDiv = document.createElement('div')
outerDiv.classList.add('outerdiv')
document.body.appendChild(outerDiv)

let innerDiv = document.createElement('div')
innerDiv.classList.add('innerdiv')
outerDiv.appendChild(innerDiv)
innerDiv.innerHTML = "clientWidth: " + innerDiv.clientWidth + "<br> offsetWidth: " +
innerDiv.offsetWidth
```

Here is what we get:

This is a little unexpected. Our innerDiv sticks out of the outerDiv even though it is inside of the outerDiv. Here is a diagram showing how the width is calculated and all the different things included:

width + padding + border (offsetWidth): 240px + 20px + 20px

width + padding (clientWidth) = 200px + 20px + 20px

clientWidth: 240
offsetWidth: 280

width: 100% = 200px

width + padding + border + margin: 280px + 20px + 20px

width: 200px

To make this problem a little better, CSS provides us with a different sizing model called `border-box` where the element, padding and border are all included in the width and height. To use it, we need to add the "`box-sizing`" property to the CSS:

```css
.outerdiv {
    box-sizing: border-box;
    width: 200px;
    border: 1px;
    border-color: yellowgreen;
    border-style: solid;
    padding: 0px;
    margin: 0px
}

.innerdiv {
    box-sizing: border-box;
    width: 100%;
    border-width: 20px;
    border-color: navy;
    border-style: solid;
    margin: 20px;
    padding: 20px;
    background-color: cyan
}
```

Let's see what that does:

Now this is much better. What happens is that when we set width: 100% for the innerDiv, with "border-box" the width included the element, the padding and the border. Since the border of the outerDiv is 1px, its actual width is 200px - 1px (left border) - 1px (right border), that is 198px. So, when we set the width of the innerDiv to 100%, it gets a width including the element, padding and border of 198px.

But the innerDiv still sticks out because of the margin. Let's get rid of the margin of the innerDiv:

```
.innerdiv {
    box-sizing: border-box;
    width: 100%;
    border-width: 20px;
    border-color: navy;
    border-style: solid;
    margin: 0px;
    padding: 20px;
    background-color: cyan
}
```

Here is what we get:

The takeaway from this section about the box model is that to make our lives easy:

- Always use box-sizing: border-box

- Avoid using margins

If we don't use margins, can you think how we would put some space between the border of the `innerDiv` and the border of the `outerDiv`? The answer is to use padding on the `outerDiv`. Let's try it out:

```css
.outerdiv {
    box-sizing: border-box;
    width: 200px;
    border: 1px;
    border-color: yellowgreen;
    border-style: solid;
    padding: 0px;
    margin: 0px;
    padding: 5px
}
```

Here is what we get:

How about that! Now that we have learned how to size things, let's move on to positioning things.

POSITIONING THINGS

There are many ways to position things on an HTML page. In this book, we will use a CSS technique called "Flexbox" to position things.

To tell the computer that you are going to use Flexbox, this is what you need to do with all your `div`s that have other `div`s in them:

```css
.containerDiv {
    display: flex
}
```

We will not go into detail on how to use Flexbox because there is a great online game that will teach you everything you need to know called Flexbox Froggy:

https://flexboxfroggy.com/

Once you finish the game, you will know everything you need to know about Flexbox. In a little bit we will use this in our game to position all the cards.

Next, let's take a short break from code and learn a little bit about how the Internet works.

CHAPTER 14: HOW THE INTERNET WORKS

O n your computer, you open the browser and type in "s1dd.com". The browser will turn that into "http://s1dd.com". This address of a website is called the "URL". What your browser does is then asks someone the directions to s1dd.com. That someone is called a DNS (Domain Name Service) server. A server is just a computer. It is called a server because it serves things to you. When your computer connects to the Internet, it is told who this DNS Server is. The DNS server then tells your computer where to find any address on the Internet. Sites on the internet are also on servers, just like your computer. This means we can turn your computer into a server!! Let's do that.

There are many different software options to turn your computer into a server. Some popular ones are Apache, IIS and Node. We will use Node here because with Node you can write all the code that you need to write for your server in JavaScript.

JAVASCRIPT ON THE SERVER

To get node, go to https://nodejs.org/ and install the version that says "Recommended For Most Users"

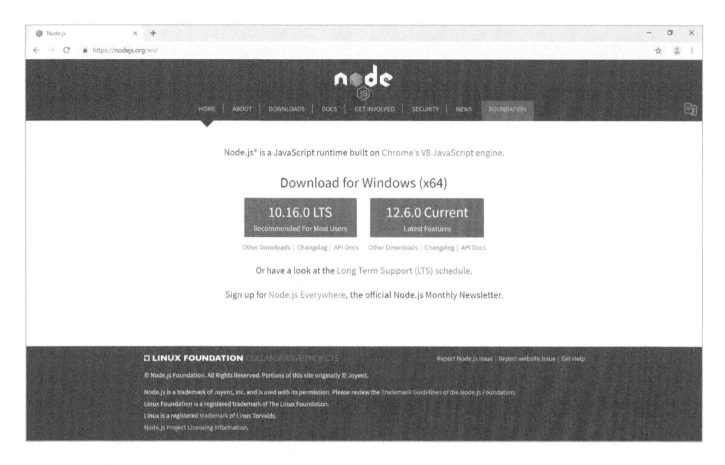

Ask a parent or friend if you need any help to install Node.

Have you ever seen a movie or TV show where you see hackers typing some commands on a computer? Generally, they are typing things in something called a terminal. VS Code has access to a terminal inbuilt into it and we will now use that to make and run our server.

To start a terminal, click New Terminal from the menu in VS Code:

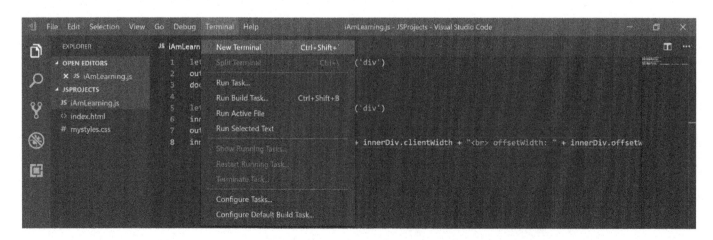

83

You will then see a terminal open in the bottom half of the screen:

Now that we have node installed, we can install all kinds of code other people have written directly from the Internet. To run our web server, we are going to install some web server software that someone has written for us. The one we are going to use for now is called "express". You can find more information about express at - http://expressjs.com/.

In the terminal, type "npm install express" and press Enter:

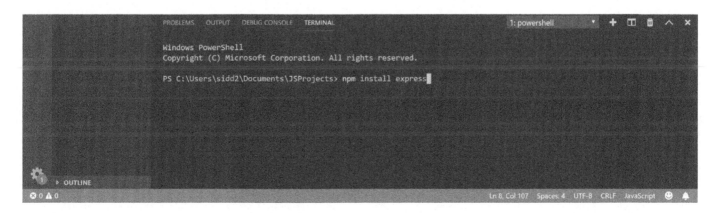

84

Now create a new file called "*server.js*"

In that file, put this code:

```javascript
// This tells node that we want to use express
const express = require('express')

// this sets up express
const app = express()

// this is the port on the computer that express will use
const port = 1337

// This tells express to send the files in current folder when someone goes to our server.
app.use(express.static('.'))

// This function is called when express is started
const callWhenServerStarted = () => {
    console.log("Listening on port " +  port)
}

// This starts the server
app.listen(port, callWhenServerStarted)
```

This code tells Node (this code runs in Node, not in the browser) that it should use the express code we just installed. It then tells it send the files from the same folder that we are in when someone goes to our server. When the server is started, it will call the function `callWhenServerStarted`.

Notice the use of `const` everywhere. This code was copied and modified from the express documentation and they follow good coding practice so they used `const` for everything that shouldn't be overwritten by something else.

85

Now let's run our server. In the terminal, type "node server.js".

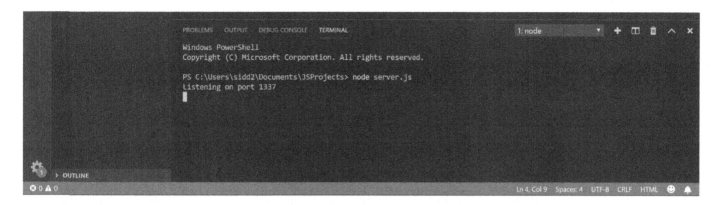

Now, our server is running. Remember what I told you about URLs and addresses. Your own computer has a very special address called localhost. Whenever you type localhost in the browser, it knows to go to a webserver on your own computer. In our server settings (see the `port` constant in the code), we typed in the port as 1337. So, to get to the server we are running, type this in the browser:

http://localhost:1337/

It will automatically load your *index.html* file. Let's see if this works:

Hurray! It did. We are now running a local web server that is serving files from a folder on our computer and we can get to it in the browser!

Now we can learn to code like real developers do.

CHAPTER 15: ORGANIZING CODE

PUTTING THINGS IN DIFFERENT FILES

As you write more and more code, your JavaScript file becomes bigger and bigger. It becomes harder and harder to read code as the file becomes bigger. To make your life easier in the future, put different things in different files. A popular way to do this is to make one file for each `class` that you have. So, in VS Code, let's make a new file called *child.js*, and put our child `class` in it.

```javascript
class Child {
    constructor(name, nerd) {
        this.name = name
        this.nerd = nerd
    }

    play(sport) {
        let div = document.createElement('div')
        div.innerHTML = this.name + ' played ' + sport
        document.body.appendChild(div)
    }
}

export default Child
```

Look at that last line – `export default Child` – that tells the browser that this file makes available ("exports") the `Child` class.

Now put the following code in our *iAmLearning.js* file:

```javascript
import Child from './child.js'

let boy1 = new Child('Jack', true)
let girl1 = new Child('Mary', false)
boy1.play('hide and seek')
girl1.play('with ' + boy1.name)
```

87

Look at the first line – `import Child from './child.js'` – this tells the browser to import whatever is exported by *child.js* into the `Child` variable. Look at the `./` in front of the `child.js` - that tells the browser to look for it in the same location as the *iAmLearning.js* file.

Imports in JavaScript are new to the language. To tell the browser that your JavaScript file imports things, you need to add the `type` property to your script tag in the HTML and give it a value of `"module"`, like shown here:

```
<html>
    <body>
        <script src="iAmLearning.js" type="module"></script>
    </body>
</html>
```

Let's see if all this worked:

It did!!

BACK TO OUR GAME

We should now put all the things we have done so far for our game into separate files. So far, we have `PokemonCard` and `Player`. Let's also make a `Game` class.

Make *pokemonCard.js*, *player.js* and *game.js* files and let's put the code we have so far in those files and add export the `class`es.

pokemonCard.js

```
class PokemonCard {
    /**
     * A pokemon card must be created with the following properties:
     * @param {String} name
     * @param {Number} HP
     * @param {String} image
     * @param {Array} attacks
     */
    constructor(name, HP, image, attacks) {
        this.name = name
        this.HP = HP
        this.image = image
        this.attacks = attacks
    }

/**
 * Show the image of this card in the div.
 * @param {HTMLDivElement} div
 */
    show(div) {
        // create the image element
        let image = document.createElement('img')

        // set the src property to the back of the card
        image.src = 'https://github.com/sgd2z/elementary-
javascript/blob/master/Chapter22/images/pokemon_card_back.jpg?raw=true'

        // put the image element in the div
        div.appendChild(image)

        const showImage = () => {
            image.removeEventListener('click', showImage)
            image.src = this.image
        }

        // add click listener
        image.addEventListener('click', showImage)
    }
}

export default PokemonCard
```

Note the documentation for the `div` parameter. It says `div` is of type `HTMLDivElement`. That is how you document HTML elements. If you want to say something is an image, you would similarly use `HTMLImageElement`.

player.js

```
import PokemonCard from './pokemonCard.js'

class Player {
    /**
    * A player has the following properties
    * @param {String} name
    * @param {Array<PokemonCard>} cards
    */
    constructor(name, cards) {
        this.name = name
        this.cards = cards
        this.score = 0
    }

    /**
    * The player should now take a turn
    */
    play() {

    }
}

export default Player
```

Note the documentation comment for the `cards` parameter. This tells VS Code to tell you that `cards` is a list of objects that are of the `PokemonCard` type.

game.js

```
import Player from './player.js'

class Game {
    constructor() {
        this.player1 = new Player("player1", [])
```

```
        this.player2 = new Player("player2", [])
    }

    start() {
    }

    getAllPokemonCards() {
    }
}

export default Game
```

CHAPTER 16: MORE ABOUT LISTS

ADDING AND REMOVING ITEMS

We already know how to add things to the end of a list using the push method. However, what if you want to remove something from a list? Or add something to the middle of list? Can you think how we would remove something with what we already know? Let's give it a shot and try to make a function to remove something from a list. One way to do it is to make a new list without that item:

```
const removeItemFromList = (list, positionToRemove) => {
    let newList = []
    let position = 0
    while (position < list.length) {
        // If the position is not the position to remove, put the item in the new list
        if (position !== positionToRemove) {
            newList.push(list[position])
        }
    }
    return newList
}
```

Don't worry, that's just an example. JavaScript lists are cool. We don't really need to write much code to work with lists.

```
Internally in JavaScript lists are made from a class called Array. Making a new list

let list = []

is the same as doing this:

let list = new Array()
```

Lists give you inbuilt ways to add and remove things from lists using a method called splice.

To remove items from a list, you call `list.splice` with what position you want to start removing at and how many things you want to remove:

```
let list = ['a', 'b', 'c', 'd', 'e']
let removedItems = list.splice(1, 2) //removedItems will contain ['b', 'c']
// list will now have ['a', 'd', 'e']
```

To add items to a list you call `list.splice` with what position you want to start adding and what you want to add. Let's add something to our list example above:

```
list.splice(1, 0, 'f', 'g')
// list will now have ['a', 'f', 'g', 'd', e']
```

Let's see if all this works

```
let div = document.createElement('div')
document.body.appendChild(div)

let list = ['a', 'b', 'c', 'd', 'e']
div.innerHTML = list
div.innerHTML = div.innerHTML + '<br>'

let removedItems = list.splice(1, 2) //removedItems will contain ['b', 'c']
div.innerHTML = div.innerHTML + removedItems
div.innerHTML = div.innerHTML + '<br>'
// list will now have ['a', 'd', 'e']
div.innerHTML = div.innerHTML + list
div.innerHTML = div.innerHTML + '<br>'

list.splice(1, 0, 'f', 'g')
// list will now have ['a', 'f', 'g', 'd', e']
div.innerHTML = div.innerHTML + list
div.innerHTML = div.innerHTML + '<br>'
```

Later in the book we will use this to shuffle a deck of cards. Stay tuned.

REMOVING ITEMS FROM A LIST IN A LOOP

Let's say we had a list - [4, 5, 6, 5, 4, 7, 7, 7, 5, 6]. Let's say we wanted to remove all numbers greater than 5 from the list. Let's try out our usual loop to do this:

```
let myList = [4, 5, 6, 5, 4, 7, 7, 7, 5, 6]
```

```
let position = 0
while (position < myList.length) {
    let item = myList[position]
    if (item > 5) {
        myList.splice(position, 1)
    }
    position = position + 1
}
div.innerHTML = div.innerHTML + myList
div.innerHTML = div.innerHTML + '<br>'
```

What we get after running this code is:

4,5,5,4,7,5

Obviously, this did not work. Can you figure out why? This is a little bit tricky. If we remove something from a list while looping through it like we did before, things get messed up. Let's say we are at position 2 in the list (the number 6) and we remove the item at position 2. Then the item at position 3 automatically moves to position 2 and then when our loop moves forward to position 3, the item that was at position 3 before gets skipped.

As our loop is running, we miss items and some of those could have been greater than 5. Can you think of a way to make this work?

One way to make this work is to not move the position from moving forward if we deleted something from the list. Here is how we would do that:

```
myList = [4, 5, 6, 5, 4, 7, 7, 7, 5, 6]
position = 0
while (position < myList.length) {
    let item = myList[position]
    if (item > 5) {
        myList.splice(position, 1)
    } else {
        position = position + 1
    }
}
div.innerHTML = div.innerHTML + myList
div.innerHTML = div.innerHTML + '<br>'
```

Another way to do that is to count backwards:

```
myList = [4, 5, 6, 5, 4, 7, 7, 7, 5, 6]
position = myList.length - 1
while (position > -1) {
    let item = myList[position]
    if (item > 5) {
        myList.splice(position, 1)
    }
    position = position - 1
}
div.innerHTML = div.innerHTML + myList
div.innerHTML = div.innerHTML + '<br>'
```

We start counting at `myList.length - 1` because that is the last item in the list. And we need to count backwards (note we did `position = position - 1`) until we reach 0. So, our condition for the loop is `position > -1`.

BACK TO OUR GAME

In our game, when a Pokémon is attacked enough to get to zero HP, we should remove it from the player's list of cards. Right now, we don't know yet when that happens, but we can definitely write the code to remove a card from a player's list:

In *player.js*:

```
import PokemonCard from './pokemonCard.js'

class Player {
    /**
     * A player has the following properties
     * @param {String} name
     * @param {Array<PokemonCard>} cards
     */
    constructor(name, cards) {
        this.name = name
        this.cards = cards
        this.score = 0
    }

    /**
     * The player should now take a turn
```

```
    */
    play() {

    }

    /**
     * remove the card at index from this.cards
     * @param {Number} index
     */
    removeCard(index) {
        this.cards.splice(index, 1)
    }

}

export default Player
```

CHAPTER 17: A LOOK AT SOME INBUILT JAVASCRIPT STUFF

A few pages ago, we talked about how JavaScript has some inbuilt stuff to help you with many things. In this chapter, we will look at two of these things: The `Math` object and the `Date class`. Both are very useful and are things you will use often.

THE MATH OBJECT

The `Math` object contains many methods to help you with all kinds of math stuff like rounding numbers, generating random numbers and many more useful functions. You can find complete information for the `Math` object here –

https://developer.mozilla.org/en-US/docs/Web/JavaScript/Reference/Global_Objects/Math

We won't talk about everything in the `Math` object in this book. We will, however, look at a few useful things that we will need in our game. The first thing we will look at is `Math.random()` - a function to generate random numbers.

```
let num = Math.random()
```

This generates a number between 0 and 1. Something like 0.329879234. Every time you call `Math.random()`, it generates a different random number. We can use for things like picking a random word from a list of words for hangman or a random number to simulate rolling dice. Or our friend who was helping make something for the teacher can use it to generate random numbers for fractions. We will use it for shuffling cards in Chapter 18 and to pick a random set of cards for the players in our game.

The problem with `Math.random()` is that it can only make random numbers between 0 and 1 like 0.3133845363142984. How do we convert that to a random number that we want which doesn't contain decimals and is between any two numbers of our choice?

Before we try to do that, let's talk about rounding. The `Math` object gives us three methods to round things:

`Math.floor` - rounds down

`Math.ceil` - rounds up

`Math.round` - rounds to the nearest integer

Now let's get back to random numbers. Let's say we need a number between 0 and 10. All we need to do is multiply `Math.random()` by 10. But this number will still have decimals. Also, it will never be 0 or 10. To get rid of the decimals, we can floor the number:

```
num = Math.floor(Math.random() * 10)
```

Now this will never produce 10. It will just get a number from 0 to 9. This is very useful for us for things like finding a random index in a list of 10 items. Remember the indexes go from 0 to 9.

Using all this information, can you think of a way to get a random number that is between 5 and 15? It should include both 5 and 15 in the numbers that it generates.

First let's see how many numbers we could possibly generate:

5,6,7,8,9,10,11,12,13,14,15

That's 11 numbers. We know we can generate 11 numbers from 0 to 10 by doing this:

```
num = Math.floor(Math.random() * 11)
```

But we need numbers between 5 and 15. So we just add 5 to our number:

```
num = Math.floor(Math.random() * 11) + 5
```

Exercise

1. Write a function to generate a random number between two numbers? See Appendix 4 for an answer.

2.   Write a function to simulate the roll of a dice?

THE DATE CLASS

Unlike `Math`, which is just a plain object, `Date` is a `class`. We can create a date using:

```
let date = new Date()
```

That creates an object with the current date and time in it. You can create an object with any date you want by passing parameters to the constructor of the date object.

```
let date = new Date ('April 1, 2019 14:30')
```

JavaScript understands that and will create a new date with that date in it.

The `Date class` also provided functions to get the day, month, year and more from any date.

Computers internally store dates as the number of milliseconds from January 1, 1970 in a time zone called UTC. To get the current time in that format we can do:

```
let startTime = Date.now()
```

Now we can do some cool things like see how long it takes a computer to do things. How long do you think it will take you to count to a million? How long do you think it will take the computer? Let's find out.

```
alert('go')
let startTime = Date.now()
let counter = 0
while (counter < 1000000) {
    counter = counter + 1
}
let endTime = Date.now()
let timeTaken = endTime - startTime
alert(timeTaken + ' milliseconds')
```

So how long was it? More, or less, than you thought? On my computer it took 7 milliseconds.

> Did you notice something strange about `Date.now()`? We called the `now` method directly on the `Date` class. We didn't make a new object of the class and call the method on that object. This kind of method that you call directly on a `class` is called a "static" method.

CHAPTER 18: PUTTING EVERYTHING TOGETHER - SHUFFLING CARDS

N ow let's do something fun. Let's make use of what we have learned so far to make and shuffle a deck of cards. This code will come in handy anytime we want to build a card game. Some of this will even be useful for our Pokémon game.

BUILDING A CARD DECK

Let's think back to the classes chapter and do the first thing we need to do – figure out how to describe a card.

What properties does a card have?

- A card has a suite (hearts, diamonds, spades or clubs)

- A number (2-10) or a type (Ace, King, Queen, Jack)

However, the value of a King is greater than that of a Queen and that of a Queen is greater than that of a Jack and that of a Jack is greater than that of a 10. We will give a Jack a value of 11, Queen a value of 12 and King a value of 13. In some games an Ace has a value greater than the king - so 14, and in some games, the Ace has a value of 1. For now, we will give it a value of one.

Knowing all this, we will give a card three properties - name or type, value and suite. Here is how we will define a Card class in a new file *card.js*

```
class Card {
    /**
     * @param {string} name Name of the card
```

```
     * @param {Number} value Value of the card
     * @param {string} suite Suite of the card
     */
    constructor(name, value, suite) {
        this.name = name
        this.value = value
        this.suite = suite
    }
}

export default Card
```

The next thing we will do is make a `Deck` class for a deck of cards. What does a deck have? All the cards of all the suites. So, in the constructor, we create and add all the cards to the deck.

```
import Card from './card.js'

class Deck {
    /**
     * Builds a deck of cards
     */
    constructor() {
        // The list of cards in the deck
        this.cards = []

        // List of Suites
        let suites = ['spades', 'hearts', 'diamonds', 'clubs']

        // List of card names. The values of each card are the index in the list + 1. Ace
is assumed to have a value of 1
        let cardNames = ['Ace', '2', '3', '4', '5', '6', '7', '8', '9', '10', 'Jack',
'Queen', 'King']

        // Loop through the suites
        let suitePosition = 0
        while (suitePosition < suites.length) {
            // Loop through all the cards for each suite
            let cardPosition = 0
            while (cardPosition < cardNames.length) {
                // Create the card
                let card = new Card(cardNames[cardPosition], cardPosition + 1,
suites[suitePosition])

                // Add the card to the list of cards in the deck
```

```
            this.cards.push(card);

            cardPosition = cardPosition + 1
        }
        suitePosition = suitePosition + 1
    }
  }
}

export default Deck
```

SHUFFLING

Next let's talk about what we really want to do. Shuffle. What is shuffling? Shuffling basically is arranging the cards is random order. There are many ways to shuffle in real life. Now we could go about implementing one of those real-life ways or we could think about a simple computer way to shuffle things. When I asked my son how he would shuffle on the computer, he said he would pick a card at random from the list and then put it back at another random position and then do that many times.

Let's write that out in steps and figure out how we would write the code for that:

- Remove a card from the deck from a random position

- Put the card back in the deck at another random position

- Do this many times

When I asked how many times, he came up with the number 100. Now let's use that and break this down into further steps:

- Do this 100 times:

    - Find a random position in the deck

    - Remove a card from there

    - Find another random position in the deck

- Put the card back in that position

Here is the code we came up with for that. Add this to your `Deck` class:

```
/**
 * Shuffle this deck by taking a card from a random position and putting it another
random position many times
 */
shuffle1() {
    let counter = 0
    // Do this 100 times
    while (counter < 100) {
        // Find a random position in the deck
        let randomIndexToRemoveFrom = Math.floor(Math.random() * this.cards.length)

        // Remove a card from there
        let removedCard = this.cards.splice(randomIndexToRemoveFrom, 1)

        // Find another random position in the deck
        let randomIndexToPutBackIn = Math.floor(Math.random() * this.cards.length)

        // Put the card back in that position
        this.cards.splice(randomIndexToPutBackIn, 0, removedCard[0])

        counter = counter + 1
    }
}
```

Look at the line to put the card back in the deck:

```
this.cards.splice(randomIndexToPutBackIn, 0, removedCard[0])
```

We use `removedCard[0]` because even though we only removed one item splice gives us back a list. Therefore, we must put the first item from that list back in. How do we know this worked? Let's go to the next section and see how we can find out.

CHAPTER 19: DEBUGGING

TRYING OUT SHUFFLING

Often you will write code that doesn't work, or you won't know whether your code worked or not. How do you find problems in your code or see what it is doing? That process is called debugging. Problems in code are called bugs. That's why finding and fixing problems is called debugging.

Let's try to use our `Deck class` from above and shuffle a deck and see if it works. Put this in your *iAmLearning.js* file:

```
import Deck from './deck.js'

let deck = new Deck()

deck.shuffle1()
```

Now go to *localhost:1337* in Chrome like before. Chrome has a debugger built into the browser. Generally, you can click Ctrl + Shift + I in Chrome and it will bring up the debugger. Here is what the debugger looks like:

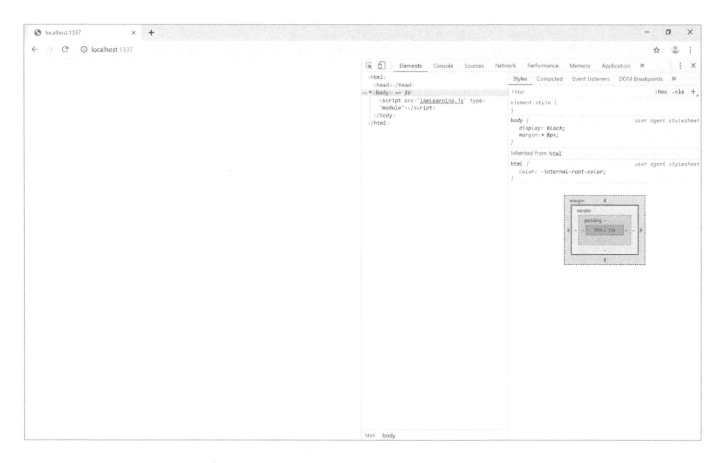

You can position the debugger wherever you want in the browser and even detach it and view it side by side outside the browser by clicking the little position icons in the menu:

For the rest of this book, I will keep the debugger at the bottom of the page. Click on the "Sources" tab in the debugger and it will show you all the files in your code.

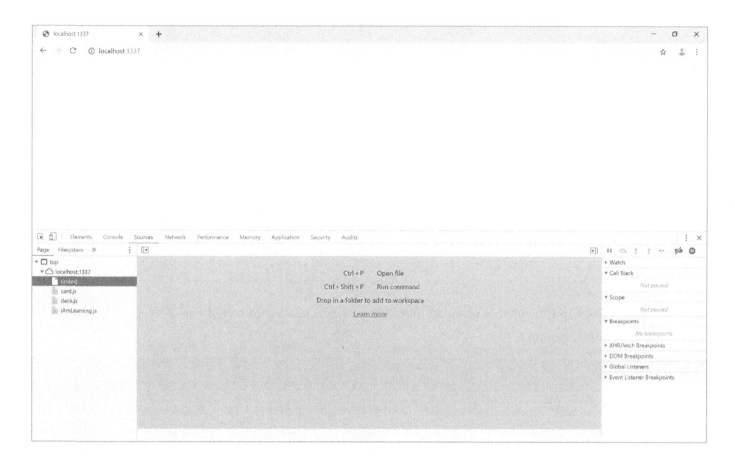

Next click the three tiny dots on the top right of the debugger and click "Show Console Drawer":

Now you will see a little place under your code files where you can write code in the browser to test things out called "Console":

You can write things to the console using an inbuilt method in JavaScript called `console.log`. Let's add one of those to our *iAmLearning.js* file:

```
import Deck from './deck.js'

let deck = new Deck()

deck.shuffle1()
console.log(deck.cards)
```

Now let's reload the page in the browser and see what happens. We now see that our list of cards shows up in the console area:

You can expand the list by clicking that tiny arrow:

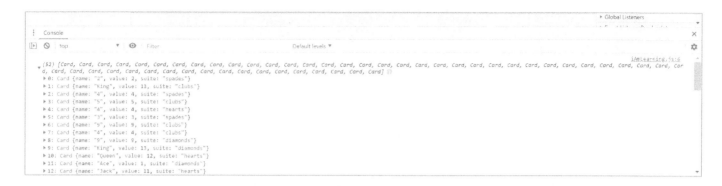

You can see that the card list is reasonably well shuffled.

OTHER WAYS TO SHUFFLE

Now let's try some more shuffling methods. One of my favorite shuffling methods is called riffle. For a riffle shuffle, you divide the deck into two equal parts then you quickly merge those two parts by leafing a few cards from each part in between cards from the other part.

Let's see if we can write the algorithm for riffle shuffle and then write the code for it.

- Divide the deck into two parts

- Loop until both parts are empty

  - Take a small random number of cards from the first part

  - Take a small random number of cards from the second part

  - Put these together

Now let's think this through. Where will we put the parts together? Maybe we should make a new list and put the parts in the new list. Then our algorithm would be:

- Divide the deck into two parts

- Make a new empty list

- Loop until both parts are empty

  - Take a small random number of cards from the first part

  - Put them in the new list

  - Take a small random number of cards from the second part

  - Put them in the new list

- The new list is now our shuffled deck

Add the following `riffle` method to your Deck class:

```
/**
 * Shuffle the deck using the riffle method
 */
riffle() {
    // Divide the deck into two parts
    // One part is in halfDeck, the other part is in deck
    let halfDeck = this.deck.splice(0, deck.length / 2)
```

```
    // Make a new empty list
    let shuffledDeck = []

    // Loop until both parts are empty
    while (halfDeck.length > 0 || this.deck.length > 0) {
        // Take a small random number (upto 4) of cards from the first part
        let randomNumber1 = Math.floor(Math.random() * 4)
        let cardsFromFirstHalf = halfDeck.splice(0, randomNumber1)

        // Put them in the new list
        let position = 0
        while (counter < cardsFromFirstHalf.length) {
            shuffledDeck.push(cardsFromFirstHalf[position])
        }

        // Take a small random number of cards from the second part
        let randomNumber2 = Math.floor(Math.random() * 4)
        let cardsFromSecondHalf = this.deck.splice(0, randomNumber2)

        // Put them in the new list
        position = 0
        while (counter < cardsFromSecondHalf.length) {
            shuffledDeck.push(cardsFromSecondHalf[position])
        }
    }

    // The new list is now our shuffled deck
    this.deck = shuffledDeck
}
```

Did you notice anything wrong with the code above? Let's change the `deck.shuffle1()` in our iAmLearning.js file to `deck.riffle()` and let's see what happens:

```
import Deck from './deck.js'
let deck = new Deck()
deck.riffle()
console.log(deck.cards)
```

Whoopsie. The code did not work ☹! The debugger shows me an error:

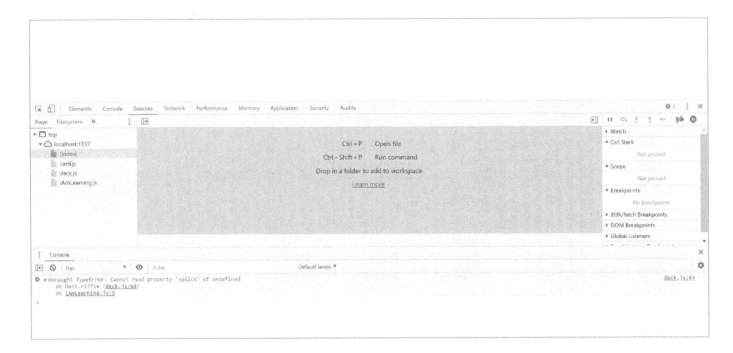

That error means that we tried to call `splice` on a variable that was not defined. The error is in the `riffle` method in `class Deck` on line 60 in *deck.js* which was called from line 4 in *iAmLearning.js*

If we click on *deck.js* in the list of files, the bad line is shown in the debugger:

If you click on the number 64 right next to the line with the red error squiggly underline, the number will be highlighted. This is called a *breakpoint*. It means, the next time you run this code, it will stop here so you can see what is happening:

Now that we have setup a breakpoint, let's reload the page and see what happens:

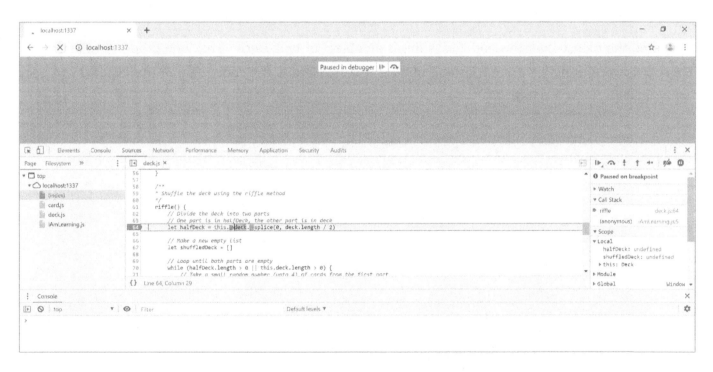

The page gets paused at that line. Now we can hover over all the variables on that line and see what is wrong.

I hovered the mouse over this and it says this is an object of type Deck. It has one property called `cards`. Oops. We were using `this.deck` instead of `this.cards`. Here is the code with all the instances of `deck` replaced with `cards` instead:

```
/**
 * Shuffle the deck using the riffle method
 */
riffle() {
    // Divide the deck into two parts
    // One part is in halfDeck, the other part is in deck
    let halfDeck = this.cards.splice(0, cards.length / 2)

    // Make a new empty list
    let shuffledDeck = []

    // Loop until both parts are empty
    while (halfDeck.length > 0 || this.cards.length > 0) {
        // Take a small random number (upto 4) of cards from the first part
        let randomNumber1 = Math.floor(Math.random() * 4)
        let cardsFromFirstHalf = halfDeck.splice(0, randomNumber1)

        // Put them in the new list
        let position = 0
```

```
        while (counter < cardsFromFirstHalf.length) {
            shuffledDeck.push(cardsFromFirstHalf[position])
        }

        // Take a small random number of cards from the second part
        let randomNumber2 = Math.floor(Math.random() * 4)
        let cardsFromSecondHalf = this.cards.splice(0, randomNumber2)

        // Put them in the new list
        position = 0
        while (counter < cardsFromSecondHalf.length) {
            shuffledDeck.push(cardsFromSecondHalf[position])
        }
    }

        // The new list is now our shuffled deck
        this.cards = shuffledDeck
    }
```

let's reload the page. When the browser stops at a breakpoint, you can click the blue play button on the page to continue. Let's see what happens when we continue:

Oh no, it is still broken ☠. This time it is telling us that a variable called cards is not defined. Oops. It should be this.cards. Let's fix it and see if it works:

To remove the breakpoint, just click on the blue highlighted number again. But now we have another problem! Still broken ✕. Oops. We called our variable `position` but, in the loop, we used `counter`. Let's fix that and see if this code works now:

```
/**
 * Shuffle the deck using the riffle method
 */
riffle() {
    // Divide the deck into two parts
    // One part is in halfDeck, the other part is in deck
    let halfDeck = this.cards.splice(0, this.cards.length / 2)

    // Make a new empty list
    let shuffledDeck = []

    // Loop until both parts are empty
    while (halfDeck.length > 0 || this.cards.length > 0) {
        // Take a small random number (upto 4) of cards from the first part
        let randomNumber1 = Math.floor(Math.random() * 4)
        let cardsFromFirstHalf = halfDeck.splice(0, randomNumber1)

        // Put them in the new list
        let position = 0
        while (position < cardsFromFirstHalf.length) {
            shuffledDeck.push(cardsFromFirstHalf[position])
        }

        // Take a small random number of cards from the second part
        let randomNumber2 = Math.floor(Math.random() * 4)
```

```
        let cardsFromSecondHalf = this.cards.splice(0, randomNumber2)

        // Put them in the new list
        position = 0
        while (position < cardsFromSecondHalf.length) {
            shuffledDeck.push(cardsFromSecondHalf[position])
        }
    }

    // The new list is now our shuffled deck
    this.cards = shuffledDeck
}
```

Nope. Still didn't work and this time the browser just got stuck and Chrome gave us a warning and automatically paused for a "potential out-of-memory crash" ☺:

If the debugger is not open, you will get this problem when that happens:

When the browser just gets stuck like that, we have probably created an infinite loop - a loop that goes on forever.

Can you tell why some loop in our function goes on forever? I'm guessing you have already figured it out. If not, look at the code below and see what was added:

```
/**
 * Shuffle the deck using the riffle method
 */
riffle() {
    // Divide the deck into two parts
    // One part is in halfDeck, the other part is in deck
    let halfDeck = this.cards.splice(0, this.cards.length / 2)

    // Make a new empty list
    let shuffledDeck = []

    // Loop until both parts are empty
    while (halfDeck.length > 0 || this.cards.length > 0) {
        // Take a small random number (upto 4) of cards from the first part
        let randomNumber1 = Math.floor(Math.random() * 4)
        let cardsFromFirstHalf = halfDeck.splice(0, randomNumber1)

        // Put them in the new list
        let position = 0
        while (position < cardsFromFirstHalf.length) {
            shuffledDeck.push(cardsFromFirstHalf[position])
```

```
            position = position + 1
        }

        // Take a small random number of cards from the second part
        let randomNumber2 = Math.floor(Math.random() * 4)
        let cardsFromSecondHalf = this.cards.splice(0, randomNumber2)

        // Put them in the new list
        position = 0
        while (position < cardsFromSecondHalf.length) {
            shuffledDeck.push(cardsFromSecondHalf[position])
            position = position + 1
        }
    }

    // The new list is now our shuffled deck
    this.cards = shuffledDeck
}
```

Yay ♘! Finally, it is working:

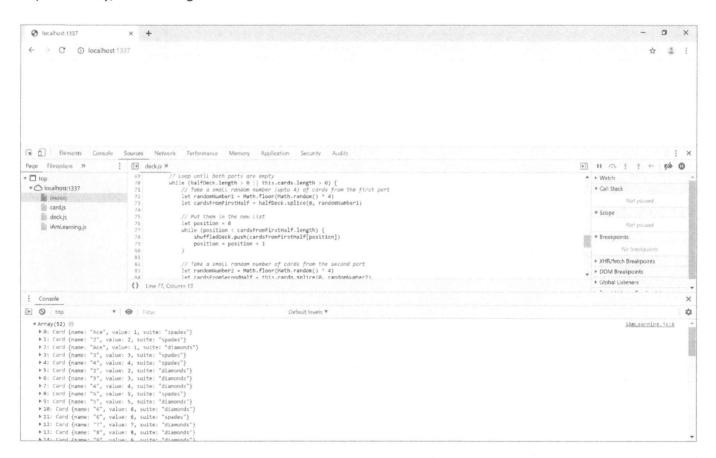

Notice, compared to our previous `shuffle`, `riffle` is not a very good method of shuffling based on the list of cards we see in the console. Generally, in real life, riffle is used before other methods of shuffling.

Here is one more method of shuffling:

```
/**
 * Another shuffle method
 */
shuffle() {
    // Create a new list
    let shuffledDeck = []

    // Loop until card list is empty
    while (this.cards.length > 0) {
        // Select a random card
        let randomIndex = Math.floor(Math.random() * this.cards.length)
        let card = this.cards.splice(randomIndex, 1)

        // Put this card in the new list
        shuffledDeck.push(card[0])
    }

    // shuffledDeck is the new list of cards
    this.cards = shuffledDeck
}
```

Which method do you think is better? `shuffle1`, `shuffle` or `riffle`? Why? Do you know any other methods of shuffling in real life? Look some up on Google. Can you write code to shuffle using those methods?

Do you know of any card games that are played with special cards? Uno is one example. Can you make Card and Deck classes for Uno?

Now we know how to find problems when our code doesn't work.

CHAPTER 20: GETTING INFORMATION AND USING IT

THE POKÉMON API

Often when you are writing code for a website in JavaScript, if you need any information you will get it from a server on the Internet. For example, if you are making the hangman game, you will get a list of words from somewhere. Many times, it is you who are keeping this information on your server. But often you get this information from other servers run by someone else. For example, you can get book information from Amazon. Generally, when you get information from a server, you get it using something called an API (Application Programming Interface).

As an example, we will write code to get information from - https://pokemontcg.io/ - a free web service to get information about Pokémon cards. Let's start with getting a list of Pokémon cards. Here is the documentation for the API - https://docs.pokemontcg.io/.

The API says that the web address of the server where you get the information from is - https://api.pokemontcg.io. You can add extra bits to the end of that address to get different information for Pokémon cards. Those extra things that you add the end of the address are called endpoints.

The endpoint to get a list of Pokémon cards is "v1/cards". So to get a list of Pokémon cards, we will use this address - https://api.pokemontcg.io/v1/cards.

> If you are not into Pokémon, maybe you can try out the steps to understand how to get data and then use it to get data about Yu-Gi-Oh cards using the Yu-Gi-Oh API here:
>
> https://db.ygoprodeck.com/api-guide/

GETTING INFORMATION FROM APIS AND A NEW KIND OF FUNCTION

JavaScript has an inbuilt method called "fetch" to get information from online APIs. Luckily for us, the Pokémon API returns information in a format that can be read in JavaScript without any conversion. Let's see how to use fetch with the Pokémon API.

```
const getPokemonList = async () => {
    let file = await fetch('https://api.pokemontcg.io/v1/cards')
    let pokemonList = await file.json()
    console.log(pokemonList)
}

getPokemonList()
```

Let's talk about all the new things in code above. The first new thing is the keyword async before the function creation. This tells the browser that the function contains things that require waiting for. In this case we need to wait for the information from the API to be fetched. async stands for asynchronous. It basically means that this function could make things happen out of order. When you run an async function, JavaScript doesn't wait for it to finish before moving on to the next line.

Next, we have the keyword await before calling the fetch function. await tells the browser that it should wait for fetch to finish and then put the result in a variable called file. This makes things happen in order instead of out of order. Adding await in front of a call to an async function tells JavaScript that it should wait for it to be finished. This means fetch is an async function!

To get the information in a way that is useful we need to tell the browser what format we are expecting the information in and to get everything in that format. In this case the format is "JSON" -> JavaScript Object Notation. This is something JavaScript can directly use as an object. Notice we used await before that line too.

fetch, async and await are relatively new to JavaScript and like many of the other things in this book do not work in Internet Explorer.

Now let's see what we got from the server:

```
const getPokemonList = async () => {
    let file = await fetch('https://api.pokemontcg.io/v1/cards')
    let pokemonList = await file.json()
```

```
      console.log(pokemonList)
}

getPokemonList()
```

Here is what is in the console log:

```
                                                                                                                              iAmLearning.js:4
▼ {cards: Array(100)}
  ▼ cards: Array(100)
    ▶ 0: {id: "dp6-90", name: "Cubone", nationalPokedexNumber: 104, imageUrl: "https://images.pokemontcg.io/dp6/90.png", imageUrlHiRes: "https://images.pokemontcg.io/dp6/90_hires.png", …}
    ▶ 1: {id: "ex14-85", name: "Windstorm", imageUrl: "https://images.pokemontcg.io/ex14/85.png", imageUrlHiRes: "https://images.pokemontcg.io/ex14/85_hires.png", supertype: "Trainer", …}
    ▶ 2: {id: "pop9-17", name: "Turtwig", nationalPokedexNumber: 387, imageUrl: "https://images.pokemontcg.io/pop9/17.png", imageUrlHiRes: "https://images.pokemontcg.io/pop9/17_hires.png", …}
    ▶ 3: {id: "xy7-4", name: "Bellossom", nationalPokedexNumber: 182, imageUrl: "https://images.pokemontcg.io/xy7/4.png", imageUrlHiRes: "https://images.pokemontcg.io/xy7/4_hires.png", …}
    ▶ 4: {id: "ex8-100", name: "Hariyama ex", nationalPokedexNumber: 297, imageUrl: "https://images.pokemontcg.io/ex8/100.png", imageUrlHiRes: "https://images.pokemontcg.io/ex8/100_hires.png", …}
    ▶ 5: {id: "xyp-XY05", name: "Xerneas", nationalPokedexNumber: 716, imageUrl: "https://images.pokemontcg.io/xyp/XY05.png", imageUrlHiRes: "https://images.pokemontcg.io/xyp/XY05_hires.png", …}
    ▶ 6: {id: "ex16-1", name: "Aggron", nationalPokedexNumber: 306, imageUrl: "https://images.pokemontcg.io/ex16/1.png", imageUrlHiRes: "https://images.pokemontcg.io/ex16/1_hires.png", …}
    ▶ 7: {id: "xyp-XY11", name: "Skiddo", nationalPokedexNumber: 672, imageUrl: "https://images.pokemontcg.io/xyp/XY11.png", imageUrlHiRes: "https://images.pokemontcg.io/xyp/XY11_hires.png", …}
    ▶ 8: {id: "dp6-107", name: "Misdreavus", nationalPokedexNumber: 200, imageUrl: "https://images.pokemontcg.io/dp6/107.png", imageUrlHiRes: "https://images.pokemontcg.io/dp6/107_hires.png", …}
    ▶ 9: {id: "xy0-14", name: "Greninja", nationalPokedexNumber: 658, imageUrl: "https://images.pokemontcg.io/xy0/14.png", imageUrlHiRes: "https://images.pokemontcg.io/xy0/14_hires.png", …}
    ▶ 10: {id: "xy0-15", name: "Clauncher", nationalPokedexNumber: 692, imageUrl: "https://images.pokemontcg.io/xy0/15.png", imageUrlHiRes: "https://images.pokemontcg.io/xy0/15_hires.png", …}
    ▶ 11: {id: "ex16-16", name: "Magneton", nationalPokedexNumber: 82, imageUrl: "https://images.pokemontcg.io/ex16/16.png", imageUrlHiRes: "https://images.pokemontcg.io/ex16/16_hires.png", …}
    ▶ 12: {id: "ex13-110", name: "Fighting Energy", imageUrl: "https://images.pokemontcg.io/ex13/110.png", imageUrlHiRes: "https://images.pokemontcg.io/ex13/110_hires.png", supertype: "Energy", …}
    ▶ 13: {id: "xy11-41", name: "Joltik", nationalPokedexNumber: 595, imageUrl: "https://images.pokemontcg.io/xy11/41.png", imageUrlHiRes: "https://images.pokemontcg.io/xy11/41_hires.png", …}
    ▶ 14: {id: "xy0-18", name: "Inkay", nationalPokedexNumber: 686, imageUrl: "https://images.pokemontcg.io/xy0/18.png", imageUrlHiRes: "https://images.pokemontcg.io/xy0/18_hires.png", …}
    ▶ 15: {id: "xy0-17", name: "Mightyena", nationalPokedexNumber: 262, imageUrl: "https://images.pokemontcg.io/xy0/17.png", imageUrlHiRes: "https://images.pokemontcg.io/xy0/17_hires.png", …}
    ▶ 16: {id: "xy0-19", name: "Pawniard", nationalPokedexNumber: 624, imageUrl: "https://images.pokemontcg.io/xy0/19.png", imageUrlHiRes: "https://images.pokemontcg.io/xy0/19_hires.png", …}
    ▶ 17: {id: "dp6-113", name: "Pineco", nationalPokedexNumber: 204, imageUrl: "https://images.pokemontcg.io/dp6/113.png", imageUrlHiRes: "https://images.pokemontcg.io/dp6/113_hires.png", …}
    ▶ 18: {id: "ex16-30", name: "Glalie", nationalPokedexNumber: 362, imageUrl: "https://images.pokemontcg.io/ex16/30.png", imageUrlHiRes: "https://images.pokemontcg.io/ex16/30_hires.png", …}
    ▶ 19: {id: "base4-112", name: "Maintenance", imageUrl: "https://images.pokemontcg.io/base4/112.png", imageUrlHiRes: "https://images.pokemontcg.io/base4/112_hires.png", supertype: "Trainer", …}
    ▶ 20: {id: "xy11-25", name: "Volcanion", nationalPokedexNumber: 721, imageUrl: "https://images.pokemontcg.io/xy11/25.png", imageUrlHiRes: "https://images.pokemontcg.io/xy11/25_hires.png", …}
    ▶ 21: {id: "xy7-27", name: "Ampharos-EX", nationalPokedexNumber: 181, imageUrl: "https://images.pokemontcg.io/xy7/27.png", imageUrlHiRes: "https://images.pokemontcg.io/xy7/27_hires.png", …}
    ▶ 22: {id: "hgss4-42", name: "Magmar", nationalPokedexNumber: 126, imageUrl: "https://images.pokemontcg.io/hgss4/42.png", imageUrlHiRes: "https://images.pokemontcg.io/hgss4/42_hires.png", …}
    ▶ 23: {id: "base4-113", name: "PlusPower", imageUrl: "https://images.pokemontcg.io/base4/113.png", imageUrlHiRes: "https://images.pokemontcg.io/base4/113_hires.png", supertype: "Trainer", …}
    ▶ 24: {id: "ex16-32", name: "Lairon", nationalPokedexNumber: 305, imageUrl: "https://images.pokemontcg.io/ex16/32.png", imageUrlHiRes: "https://images.pokemontcg.io/ex16/32_hires.png", …}
    ▶ 25: {id: "bw1-105", name: "Grass Energy", imageUrl: "https://images.pokemontcg.io/bw1/105.png", imageUrlHiRes: "https://images.pokemontcg.io/bw1/105_hires.png", supertype: "Energy", …}
    ▶ 26: {id: "base5-82", name: "Potion Energy", imageUrl: "https://images.pokemontcg.io/base5/82.png", imageUrlHiRes: "https://images.pokemontcg.io/base5/82_hires.png", supertype: "Energy", …}
    ▶ 27: {id: "xy11-99", name: "Captivating Poké Puff", imageUrl: "https://images.pokemontcg.io/xy11/99.png", imageUrlHiRes: "https://images.pokemontcg.io/xy11/99_hires.png", supertype: "Trainer", …}
```

We got an object that has a cards property with a list of 100 objects in it with properties about individual Pokémon cards. Now let's go back to the documentation page for the API - https://docs.pokemontcg.io/ - and try and figure out how to get more cards and only Pokémon monster cards.

According to the documentation, we can get only Pokémon cards and not Trainer or Energy cards by using the *supertype*:

supertype	The supertype of the card. Either Pokémon, Trainer, or Energy.

Let's talk a little bit about Internet addresses aka URLs. URLs are made up of 4 parts. Let's look the URL that we will use get only monster cards:

This is the URL: `https://api.pokemontcg.io/v1/cards?supertype=Pokémon`

Here are the 4 parts of the URL:

Protocol: `https://` - The method that your browser uses to talk to the server

Hostname: `api.pokemontcg.io` - The address of the server

Path: `/v1/cards` - Where to go on the server

Query String: `?supertype=Pokémon` - Data to give the server

The query string starts with a "?". Our list only got us a hundred cards. There are thousands of Pokémon cards. We need to look at the documentation and figure out how to get more cards. The documentation tells us that we can get up to a thousand cards at a time using the parameter `pageSize` and we can get to more "pages" of cards using the `page` parameter. Here is how we would use the `page` and `pageSize` parameters:

```
https://api.pokemontcg.io/v1/cards?supertype=Pokémon&page=1&pageSize=1000
```

Notice the query string: `?supertype=Pokémon&page=1&pageSize=1000`

We use "&" to separate all the parameters. In this case we have three parameters, `supertype`, `page` and `pageSize`. To get to the next 1000 Pokémon we use 2 for the `page` like this:

```
https://api.pokemontcg.io/v1/cards?supertype=Pokémon&page=2&pageSize=1000
```

I checked to see how many pages we can get, and it turns out we can get up to page 10. So, there are nearly 10,000 Pokémon cards in that API. We can build a loop that fetches data 10 times and builds a list of all the Pokémon cards or we can find a different way to get a smaller number of cards using some of the other options in the API. For our game we only need a small number of random cards and it would be nice not to wait for so many large data requests from a server. It would slow down the loading of our game if the player doesn't have very fast Internet.

Can you think of any ways to do this? Here is one way:

- We will first select a page randomly

- Then from that page we will select the Pokémon we need

Since we know there are 10 pages, to choose a random page, we need to generate a random number between 1 and 10. Luckily, we already know how to do that. We will use the `randomBetween` function from Appendix 4 to make this happen:

```
const getPokemonList = async () => {
    let randomPage = randomBetween(1, 10)
```

```
    let file = await fetch('https://api.pokemontcg.io/v1/cards?supertype=Pokémon&page=' +
randomPage + '&pageSize=1000')
    let pokemonList = await file.json()
    console.log(pokemonList)
}

getPokemonList()
```

Look at the code above and see how we used the `randomPage` variable to make the URL that we need to get the cards from.

Yay! That worked:

Now we have a list of 1000 Pokémon to choose from.

Can you think of any other ways to get Pokémon by reading the documentation that don't involve getting everything?

MORE ABOUT ASYNC FUNCTIONS

Before we move on, there are some things to know about `async` functions. If your `async` function returns results, you can only use them in another `async` function, and you must put `await` in when you try to use the result. For example, if we wanted to get the Pokémon list and use it to do something, we would have to do something like this:

```
const getPokemonList = async () => {
    let randomPage = randomBetween(1, 10)
    let file = await fetch('https://api.pokemontcg.io/v1/cards?supertype=Pokémon&page=' +
randomPage + '&pageSize=1000')
    let pokemonList = await file.json()
    // the cards are in the cards property
```

```
    return pokemonList.cards
}

const doSomethingCoolWithPokemonList = async () => {
    let pokemonList = await getPokemonList()
    // Do Something Cool Here with the list
    // …
}
```

The reason we can't use the result of `async` functions outside other `async` functions is that internally in JavaScript, `async` functions don't return the actual value. They return a "promise" that they will get you the actual value when the function finishes all the work to get the value. The `await` keyword tells JavaScript to wait for the function to finish what it has "promised" and then gives you the real return value.

```
There are different ways to use promises in JavaScript. Using async and await is the easiest to
read. You will often find that people use the "then" function:

const getPokemonListWithoutAsyncAwait = () => {
    let randomPage = randomBetween(1, 87)
    const gotResults = (pokemonList) => {
        console.log(pokemonList)
    }
    const gotFile = (file) => {
        file.json().then(gotResults)
    }
    fetch('https://api.pokemontcg.io/v1/cards?supertype=Pokémon&page='  +  randomPage  +
'&pageSize=1000').then(gotFile)
}

Note the complicated use of function nesting and functions as parameters to other functions.
This code quickly gets hard to read and you can also not easily return results. How will you get
the results from the gotResults function

const gotResults = (pokemonList) => {
    console.log(pokemonList)
}

into the getPokemonListWithoutAsyncAwait function and return it? The simple answer is that you
cannot. You will have to make more functions and call those functions. In fact, if you read code
online, people will use functions without names called anonymous functions and then nest those
like this, making code extremely complicated:

const getPokemonListWithoutAsyncAwait = () => {
    let randomPage = randomBetween(1, 87)
    fetch('https://api.pokemontcg.io/v1/cards?supertype=Pokémon&page='  +  randomPage  +
'&pageSize=1000').then((file) => {
```

```
        file.json().then((pokemonList) => {
            console.log(pokemonList)
        })
    })
}
```

For your own sanity, just use async and await and if you see such code online that uses then instead, convert it to async and await before using it.

One thing you might ask is that how did I know that we need to use async and await with fetch? The documentation at MDN told me that fetch returns a promise:

https://developer.mozilla.org/en-US/docs/Web/API/Fetch_API/Using_Fetch

What about class methods? Can they be async? Sure thing! Only the constructor cannot be async.

BACK TO OUR GAME

Let's make a PokemonAPI class that gets us Pokémon cards and then we can create some PokemonCard objects from them.

If our getPokemonList function was part of the PokemonAPI class, here is how it would be:

```
import PokemonCard from './pokemonCard.js'

class PokemonAPI {
    /**
     * Gets information about 1000 Pokemon cards by selecting a random page from the
pokemon API full of 1000 cards
     */
    async getPokemonList() {
        // The API has 10 pages. Choose a random page
        let randomPage = randomBetween(1, 10)

        // Get the information from the API
        let file = await
fetch('https://api.pokemontcg.io/v1/cards?supertype=Pokemon&page=' + randomPage +
'&pagesize=1000')
        let pokemonList = await file.json()

        // the cards are in the cards property
```

```
        return pokemonList.cards
    }
}

export default PokemonAPI
```

Now let's see how we can create some Pokémon cards with the information from this API. Here is what we will do:

- Get some number of random cards from this list

- Make new `PokemonCard` objects from those cards

Let's see what is in the data we get for each card:

Looks like we have a lot of information. We can just select what we need to make our card objects. Read the code below and see if you can understand it:

```
/**
 * Gets a random selection of Pokemon cards
 * @param {Number} number the number of cards to get
 */
async getRandomPokemonCards(number) {
    // Get cards using the API
    let pokemonList = await this.getPokemonList()

    // Create a list
    let pokemonCards = []
```

```
        // Create a loop to get "number" cards
        let counter = 0
        while(counter < number) {
            // select a random card
            let randomIndex = randomBetween(0, pokemonList.length)
            let pokemon = pokemonList[randomIndex]

            // create a PokemonCard object from the card to use in the game
            let pokemonCard = new PokemonCard(pokemon.name, pokemon.hp, pokemon.imageUrl,
pokemon.attacks)

            // add the card to our list
            pokemonCards.push(pokemonCard)

            counter = counter + 1
        }


        console.log(pokemonCards)
        return pokemonCards
    }
```

Let's see if this works. Here is the entire code for the `PokemonAPI class` including a way to test it:

```
import PokemonCard from './pokemonCard.js'

/**
 * Generates a random number between number1 and number2
 * @param {Number} number1 an integer
 * @param {Number} number2 an integer
 */
const randomBetween = (number1, number2) => {
    //calculate the range both numbers inclusive
    let range = number2 - number1 + 1
    // generate a random number in the range and shift it by number 1
    let randomNumber = Math.floor(Math.random() * range) + number1
    return randomNumber
}


class PokemonAPI {
    /**
     * Gets information about 1000 Pokemon cards by selecting a random page from the
pokemon API full of 1000 cards
     */
    async getPokemonList() {
```

```
        // The API has 10 pages. Choose a random page
        let randomPage = randomBetween(1, 10)

        // Get the information from the API
        let file = await
fetch('https://api.pokemontcg.io/v1/cards?supertype=Pokemon&page=' + randomPage +
'&pagesize=1000')
        let pokemonList = await file.json()

        // the cards are in the cards property
        return pokemonList.cards
    }

    /**
     * Gets a random selection of Pokemon cards
     * @param {Number} number the number of cards to get
     */
    async getRandomPokemonCards(number) {
        // Get cards using the API
        let pokemonList = await this.getPokemonList()

        // Create a list
        let pokemonCards = []

        // Create a loop to get "number" cards
        let counter = 0
        while(counter < number) {
            // select a random card
            let randomIndex = randomBetween(0, pokemonList.length)
            let pokemon = pokemonList[randomIndex]

            // create a PokemonCard object from the card to use in the game
            let pokemonCard = new PokemonCard(pokemon.name, pokemon.hp, pokemon.imageUrl,
pokemon.attacks)

            // add the card to our list
            pokemonCards.push(pokemonCard)

            counter = counter + 1
        }

        console.log(pokemonCards)
        return pokemonCards
```

```
    }

}

// Testing to see if this works
let pokemonAPI = new PokemonAPI();
pokemonAPI.getRandomPokemonCards(10);

export default PokemonAPI
```

Put all the code for the `PokemonAPI class` in a *pokemonApi.js* file. Change the *index.html* file to be this:

```
<html>
    <body>
        <script src="pokemonApi.js" type="module"></script>
    </body>
</html>
```

Let's see if all this worked:

It did! We can now get some random Pokémon cards to use in our game!! Let's take a closer look at the `PokemonAPI class` above. There are no `class` variables that we store. The only time we use `this` is to call some other `class` method. Also, there is no need to have multiple objects of the `PokemonAPI` class. Everyone can use the same object. When we run into something like this, we don't need to make a `class`. Remember the Math object? We can just make the `PokemonAPI` a simple object instead of a `class`:

```
const PokemonAPI = {
    /**
    * Gets information about 1000 Pokemon cards by selecting a random page from the
pokemon API full of 1000 cards
    */
    getPokemonList: async () => {
        // The API has 10 pages. Choose a random page
        let randomPage = randomBetween(1, 10)
```

```
        // Get the information from the API
        let file = await
fetch('https://api.pokemontcg.io/v1/cards?supertype=Pokemon&page=' + randomPage +
'&pagesize=1000')
        let pokemonList = await file.json()

        // the cards are in the cards property
        return pokemonList.cards
    },

    /**
    * Gets a random selection of Pokemon cards
    * @param {Number} number the number of cards to get
    */
    getRandomPokemonCards: async (number) => {
        // Get cards using the API
        let pokemonList = await PokemonAPI.getPokemonList()

        // Create a list
        let pokemonCards = []

        // Create a loop to get "number" cards
        let counter = 0
        while (counter < number) {
            // select a random card
            let randomIndex = randomBetween(0, pokemonList.length)
            let pokemon = pokemonList[randomIndex]

            // create a PokemonCard object from the card to use in the game
            let pokemonCard = new PokemonCard(pokemon.name, pokemon.hp, pokemon.imageUrl,
pokemon.attacks)

            // add the card to our list
            pokemonCards.push(pokemonCard)

            counter = counter + 1
        }

        console.log(pokemonCards)
        return pokemonCards
    }
}
```

```
// Testing to see if this works
PokemonAPI.getRandomPokemonCards(10)

export default PokemonAPI
```

Notice how we defined methods in the object? Pretty much the same as how object properties are defined. Basically, functions can be properties of objects.

CHAPTER 21: TIMERS AND WAITS

Before we move on to getting deeper into our game, one thing we need to learn is how to make the computer wait for some time before doing something. This is useful because computers do things so fast sometimes that you won't even know when they're done. So, for something like our card game, for example, if the computer takes a turn, it would be finished and done so fast that you won't even be able to see what card it played. So, if we want to show the card on the screen for some time, we must make the computer wait for some time.

JavaScript provides a function for that called setTimeout. Here is how to use it:

```
const doThisAfterTenSeconds = () => {
    alert("10 seconds are up")
}
```

```
// call doThisAfterTenSeconds after 10 seconds
let timeout = setTimeout(doThisAfterTenSeconds, 10000)
```

Notice that `setTimeout` has two parameters. The first is what function to call and the second after how long to call it. The second parameter is in milliseconds. 1 second is 1000 milliseconds. So, 10 seconds is 10,000 milliseconds. That means that the alert will happen after 10 seconds. Let's say something happens and you want to cancel the `setTimeout`, you can do that using a function called `clearTimeout`. Here is sample code that cancels the 10 second timeout after 5 seconds:

```
const doThisAfterTenSeconds = () => {
    alert("10 seconds are up")
}

// call doThisAfterTenSeconds after 10 seconds
let timeout = setTimeout(doThisAfterTenSeconds, 10000)

const doThisAfterFiveSeconds = () => {
    clearTimeout(timeout)
    alert("5 seconds are up")
}

let timeout2 = setTimeout(doThisAfterFiveSeconds, 5000)
```

Run the code above and verify that the 10 second timeout never happens.

Another thing that is useful is doing something again and again after a certain amount of time. For example, if you were making a clock or a countdown timer and wanted to show it, JavaScript as a function called `setInterval`. Here is how to use it:

```
// create a div to show the countdown
let countdownDiv = document.createElement('div')
document.body.appendChild(countdownDiv)

// Put the number of seconds to countdown in the div
let numberOfSecondsToCountdown = 10
countdownDiv.innerHTML = numberOfSecondsToCountdown

// define a variable for setInterval.
// We need to define it here so that we can use this in the countDown function
let intervalId

const countDown = () => {
    // decrease the countdown time
```

```
    numberOfSecondsToCountdown = numberOfSecondsToCountdown - 1

    // update the div with the number of seconds remaining
    countdownDiv.innerHTML = numberOfSecondsToCountdown

    // Stop counting when we reach zero
    if (numberOfSecondsToCountdown === 0) {
        clearInterval(intervalId)
    }
}

// Call the countdown function every second
intervalId = setInterval(countDown, 1000)
```

As an exercise, can you think of a way to make a countdown timer using `setTimeout` instead of `setInterval`? Look in appendix 5 for an answer.

USING TIMEOUTS WITH AWAIT

If we look at both `setInterval` and `setTimeout`, we see that they both call a function after some time. So, if we had to do something after a few seconds or just make our code wait, we'd have to make multiple functions. What if we could just wait a few seconds in our code like this:

```
await numberOfSeconds(5)
```

Let's see how we can make that happen because it will be useful in our game and will also be useful for many other things in the future.

Remember what we need to make `await` work? An `async` function. Remember how `async` functions work? They return promises. We can make a regular function into an `async` function by making it return a promise. Here is the code to do that:

```
/**
 * Function to wait a given number of seconds
 * @param {Number} secondsToWait number of seconds to wait
 */
let numberOfSeconds = (secondsToWait) => {
    /**
     * @param {Function} keepPromise When this function is called, Javascript know that
you finished doing what you promised
```

```
     */
    let promiser = (keepPromise) => {
        /**
         * This function is the one that is called after waiting the number of seconds
required
         */
        let functionToCallAfterSeconds = () => {
            // We are done waiting so we finished doing what we promised.
            keepPromise()
        }
        // Wait for secondsToWait and call functionToCallAfterSeconds
        setTimeout(functionToCallAfterSeconds, secondsToWait * 1000)
    }

    // Create a promise object and return it. This turns this function into an async
function
    let promise = new Promise(promiser)
    return promise
}
```

Let's figure out what is going on in the function. Look at the last few lines. We are returning a promise. When you create a `Promise` object in JavaScript, you give it a function as a parameter. In our case we used a function called `promiser`. That function also takes a function as a parameter. In our case we used a function called `keepPromise`. Now all we need to do when we are done with whatever we are doing is call the `keepPromise` function.

How do we use this now? Here is code that waits 5 seconds and then alters that it waited 5 seconds:

```
let waitFor5Seconds = async () => {
    await numberOfSeconds(5)
    alert('waited 5 seconds')
}

waitFor5Seconds()
```

While the code to convert `setTimeout` to be used with an `await` is quite complicated, it will be very useful in our game. As we use it in the game you will see why it is so useful compared to directly using timeouts.

CHAPTER 22: LET'S FINISH OUR GAME!

B efore we dive deeper into finishing our game, let's do a quick recap of what we know so far. Then we will finalize the rules of our game. After that we will get all the code we have written so far to build all the game objects and start building on it to finish the game.

QUICK RECAP

- We know how to make variables, classes, functions, loops, lists and objects in JavaScript. We've used that to create several things for our game already.

- We know how to create and put things on an HTML page and style them. We've used that to show a card image on the screen.

- We know how to detect when the user interacts with them and do something. We've used that to flip a card on the screen when the user clicks on it.

- We also know how to get things from APIs like the Pokémon API.

- We know about some inbuilt JavaScript stuff like Math, Date and timer functions. We've used some of this to choose random cards from the information we got from the API.

MORE ABOUT OUR GAME

Now that we know nearly everything we need to know about our game, let's see if we can use all that and finish making our Pokémon card game. Here are the rules of the game:

- There are two players.

- Each player gets some random Pokémon cards that are face down

- The players then each select a card by clicking a card.

- Then the computer will choose a random attack that the Pokémon can make for each player

- The hit points of the opposite player's card will reduce by the number in the attack

- When a Pokémon's hit points go to zero, that player clicks on another card

- The last player with cards left wins

Generally, for a project it makes a lot of sense to do a lot more planning before we write any actual code, but we've been writing a lot of code for our game as we learned. So, we will use what we have created so far and add more to finish our game.

THE GAME OBJECTS WE HAVE SO FAR

From Chapter 15, PokemonCard

From Chapter 20, PokemonAPI

From Chapter 16, Player

From Chapter 15, Game

Since we have created some of those classes, we have learnt a lot more things. Let's make a new folder for our game and start making our files from scratch and we will copy whatever code we need from what we have done before.

In our new folder, let's make our *index.html* file:

```html
<html>
    <head>
        <link rel="stylesheet" href="styles.css"></link>
    </head>
```

```
    <body>
        <script src="game.js" type="module"></script>
    </body>
</html>
```

Now let's make a *game.js* file with our `Game class` in it. Instead of exporting the `class` like we did in Chapter 15, let's just make a `pokemonGame` object and start the game by calling `pokemonGame.start()`.

```
class Game {
    constructor() {
        this.player1 = new Player("player1", [])
        this.player2 = new Player("player2", [])
    }

    start() {

    }
}

let pokemonGame = new Game()
pokemonGame.start()
```

Now let's make a *player.js* file and put our `Player class` in it:

```
import PokemonCard from './pokemonCard.js'

class Player {
    /**
    * A player has the following properties
    * @param {String} name
    * @param {Array<PokemonCard>} cards
    */
    constructor(name, cards) {
        this.name = name
        this.cards = cards
        this.score = 0
    }

    /**
    * The player should now take a turn
    */
    play() {

    }
```

```
    /**
     * remove the card at index from this.cards
     * @param {Number} index
     */
    removeCard(index) {
        this.cards.splice(index, 1)
    }
}

export default Player
```

Next comes our `PokemonCard` class in *pokemonCard.js*:

```
class PokemonCard {
    /**
     * A pokemon card must be created with the following properties:
     * @param {String} name
     * @param {Number} HP
     * @param {String} image
     * @param {Array} attacks
     */
    constructor(name, HP, image, attacks) {
        this.name = name
        this.HP = HP
        this.image = image
        this.attacks = attacks
    }


    /**
     * Show the image of this card in the div.
     * @param {HTMLDivElement} div
     */
    show(div) {
        // create the image element
        let image = document.createElement('img')

        // set the src property to the back of the card
        image.src = 'https://github.com/sgd2z/elementary-
javascript/blob/master/Chapter22/images/pokemon_card_back.jpg?raw=true'

        // put the image element in the div
        div.appendChild(image)
```

```
        const showImage = () => {
            image.removeEventListener('click', showImage)
            image.src = this.image
        }

        // add click listener
        image.addEventListener('click', showImage)
    }
}

export default PokemonCard
```

The last thing that we have made before that we need in our game is the `PokemonAPI` object in *pokemonAPI.js*:

```
import PokemonCard from './pokemonCard.js'

/**
* Generates a random number between number1 and number2
* @param {Number} number1 an integer
* @param {Number} number2 an integer
*/
const randomBetween = (number1, number2) => {
    //calculate the range both numbers inclusive
    let range = number2 - number1 + 1
    // generate a random number in the range and shift it by number 1
    let randomNumber = Math.floor(Math.random() * range) + number1
    return randomNumber
}

const PokemonAPI = {
    /**
    * Gets information about 1000 Pokemon cards by selecting a random page from the
pokemon API full of 1000 cards
    */
    getPokemonList: async () => {
        // The API has 10 pages. Choose a random page
        let randomPage = randomBetween(1, 10)

        // Get the information from the API
        let file = await
fetch('https://api.pokemontcg.io/v1/cards?supertype=Pokemon&page=' + randomPage +
'&pagesize=1000')
        let pokemonList = await file.json()
```

```
        // the cards are in the cards property
        return pokemonList.cards
    },

    /**
     * Gets a random selection of Pokemon cards
     * @param {Number} number the number of cards to get
     */
    getRandomPokemonCards: async (number) => {
        // Get cards using the API
        let pokemonList = await PokemonAPI.getPokemonList()

        // Create a list
        let pokemonCards = []

        // Create a loop to get "number" cards
        let counter = 0
        while (counter < number) {
            // select a random card
            let randomIndex = randomBetween(0, pokemonList.length)
            let pokemon = pokemonList[randomIndex]

            // create a PokemonCard object from the card to use in the game
            let pokemonCard = new PokemonCard(pokemon.name, pokemon.hp, pokemon.imageUrl,
pokemon.attacks)

            // add the card to our list
            pokemonCards.push(pokemonCard)

            counter = counter + 1
        }

        console.log(pokemonCards)
        return pokemonCards
    }

}

export default PokemonAPI
```

STARTING THE GAME

Now let's get started making everything work together. Important changes made within existing methods or functions are highlighted so we can see what changed.

What should we do when our game starts? Instead of setting up the players in the `constructor` like we did before, we need to set them up in the `start` method because we need to get cards and then assign those cards to each player. Also, once the game is over, we might want to start a new game and we can't call the `constructor` again. Let's see if we can get some number of random cards for each player and then create a player with those cards. For the time being let's assume each player gets 9 cards. See if you can do this yourself. Here is one way to do this in *game.js*:

```javascript
import Player from './player.js'
import PokemonAPI from './pokemonAPI.js'

class Game {
    /**
    * Start the game.
    * Get cards, create players.
    */
    async start() {
        let player1Cards = await PokemonAPI.getRandomPokemonCards(9)
        let player2Cards = await PokemonAPI.getRandomPokemonCards(9)
        this.player1 = new Player('Player 1', player1Cards)
        this.player2 = new Player('Player 2', player2Cards)
    }
}

let pokemonGame = new Game()
pokemonGame.start()
```

LAYOUT OF THE GAME

Before we move forward, let's see how we will organize everything on the screen. Generally, when making software applications, designers create something called a wireframe for your application. This is basically a line drawing of what your application will look like. It can be something as simple as this:

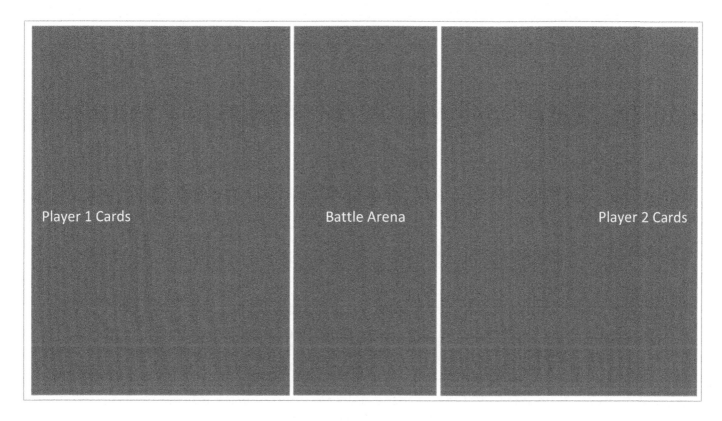

Let's say we wanted to do something like this. Can you think how we would do this?

First thing we need is three divs, one for player 1, one for player 2, and one for the arena. Let's create these divs in the constructor of our Game class because we will keep using these same divs over and over and don't need to keep creating new ones. Remember from chapter 13 how we are going to position these divs?

We will use Flexbox. To use Flexbox, we will need to put all these divs inside a main container div. Let's create all the divs and put them on the page:

```
/**
 * Setup all the things we need for the game
 */
constructor() {
    // create the divs for the players and the battle arena
    this.player1Div = document.createElement('div')
    this.player1Div.id = "player1div"

    this.player2Div = document.createElement('div')
    this.player2Div.id = "player2div"

    this.battleArena = document.createElement('div')
```

```
        this.battleArena.id = "battleArena"

        // create the main container div
        let mainDiv = document.createElement('div')
        mainDiv.id = "maindiv"

        // add the player and the battle arena divs to the the main div
        mainDiv.appendChild(this.player1Div)
        mainDiv.appendChild(this.battleArena)
        mainDiv.appendChild(this.player2Div)

        // show the main div
        document.body.appendChild(mainDiv)
    }
```

Now let's add a method to the `Player` class to show all the cards for the player. Since our `PokemonCard` class already has a `show` method, we can just use that for all the cards. Here is one way to this:

```
/**
 * Show all the cards in the div
 * @param {HTMLDivElement} div
 */
showcards(div) {
    let position = 0
    while(position < this.cards.length) {
        let card = this.cards[position]
        card.show(div)
        position = position + 1
    }
}
```

And let's show the cards as soon as the player is created in the `Player` constructor. This means that the `Player` constructor also needs a `div` parameter. And then we create the player objects in the game, we will have to pass that in:

In *player.js*:

```
/**
 * A player has the following properties
 * @param {String} name
 * @param {Array<PokemonCard>} cards
 * @param {HTMLDivElement} div The div to show the cards in
 */
constructor(name, cards, div) {
```

```
        this.name = name
        this.cards = cards
        this.score = 0
        this.showcards(div)
    }
```

In *game.js*:

```
    /**
     * Start the game.
     * Get cards, create players.
     */
    async start() {
        let player1Cards = await PokemonAPI.getRandomPokemonCards(9)
        let player2Cards = await PokemonAPI.getRandomPokemonCards(9)
        this.player1 = new Player('Player 1', player1Cards, this.player1Div)
        this.player2 = new Player('Player 2', player2Cards, this.player2Div)
    }
```

Let's see if all of this worked. Copy our *server.js* file from Chapter 14 into the folder for the game:

```
// This tells node that we want to use express
const express = require('express')

// this sets up express
const app = express()

// this is the port on the computer that express will use
const port = 1337

// This tells express to send the files in current folder when someone goes to our server.
app.use(express.static('.'))

// This function is called when express is started
const callWhenServerStarted = () => {
    console.log("Listening on port " +  port)
}

// This starts the server
app.listen(port, callWhenServerStarted)
```

Open the terminal. Make sure you are in the correct folder in the terminal. Run "npm install express". When that is done, run "node server.js". Then go to http://localhost:1337 in the browser.

Looks like it worked to show the cards on the screen:

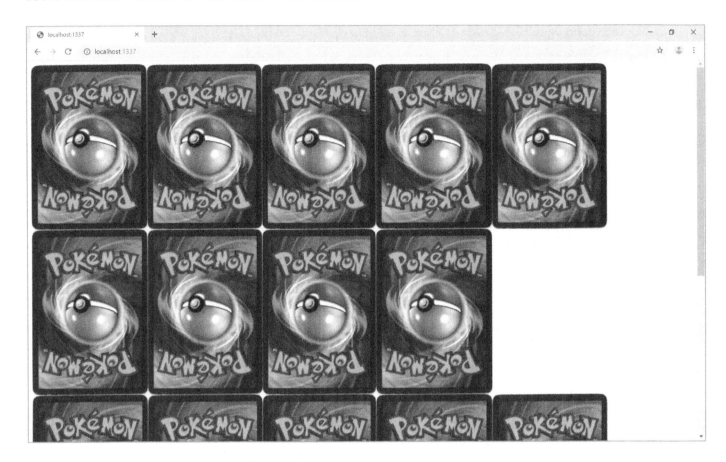

They are not exactly positioned the way we want them. Now let's see if we can use flexbox to make that happen. If we look at the wireframe drawing it looks like the play `div`s are a bit larger than the arena. Let's assume widths of 35% for each of the player `div`s, that leaves 30% for the battle arena. Let's make the margins 0 for everything because we know that margins cause problems from Chapter 13. Here is what to put in the *styles.css* file:

```css
#maindiv {
    display: flex;
    justify-content: space-between;
    margin: 0px;
    width: 100%;
}

#player1div {
    margin: 0px;
    width: 35%
}
```

```
#player2div {
    margin: 0px;
    width: 35%
}

#battleArena {
    margin: 0px;
    width: 30%
}
```

Let's see what that gets us:

That doesn't look very nice. Here is a wireframe of what the cards should look like in each player `div`:

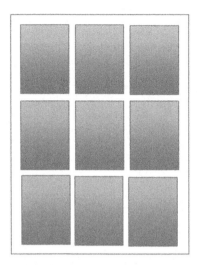

To make this happen, we need to make sure that we can fit three images in a row and three images in a column.

This means that the maximum width and maximum height of the images is 33%. However, there is also the question of the space between the cards. We can't just squish them all together. So, let's make the maximum width and height 30% and add a 1% padding.

For this we will need to add a CSS class to the card image in the PokemonCard show method and then add styles to that CSS class:

In *pokemonCard.js*:

```
/**
 * Show the image of this card in the div.
 * @param {HTMLDivElement} div
 */
show(div) {
    // create the image element
    let image = document.createElement('img')
    image.classList.add('cardImage')

    // set the src property to the back of the card
    image.src = 'https://github.com/sgd2z/elementary-
javascript/blob/master/Chapter22/images/pokemon_card_back.jpg?raw=true'

    // put the image element in the div
    div.appendChild(image)

    const showImage = () => {
        image.removeEventListener('click', showImage)
        image.src = this.image
    }

    // add click listener
    image.addEventListener('click', showImage)
}
```

In the stylesheet:

```
#maindiv {
    display: flex;
    justify-content: space-between;
```

```
        margin: 0px;
        width: 100%;
        height: 100%;
}

#player1div {
        margin: 0px;
        width: 35%;
}

#player2div {
        margin: 0px;
        width: 35%;
}

#battleArena {
        margin: 0px;
        width: 30%
}

.cardImage {
        max-width: 30%;
        max-height: 30%;
        padding: 1%;
}
```

Notice we also made the height 100% for the `maindiv`. Let's see what that gets us:

Resize the browser window and see that all the cards fit on the page properly no matter what the size of your browser window is. That is sweet, right!

There is still one small problem. Player 2's card images have more space on the right side than Player 1's. That is because by default everything is aligned left in CSS. If we align Player 2's images right, that will make everything look even. Here is how to do that in *styles.css*:

```
#player2div {
    margin: 0px;
    width: 35%;
    text-align: right
}
```

Here is what happens with that:

Remember, we already have the code to show Pokémon card images when we click on the cards. Let's see if that works by clicking around on the cards:

It does!!

GAME PLAY

Turns

Now we're all setup to start making the game playable. For the time being let's assume that Player 1 always goes first. When the game starts, we tell Player 1 to take their turn by calling the `play` function of the player. In *game.js*:

```
/**
 * Start the game.
 * Get cards, create players.
 */
async start() {
    let player1Cards = await PokemonAPI.getRandomPokemonCards(9)
    let player2Cards = await PokemonAPI.getRandomPokemonCards(9)
    this.player1 = new Player('Player 1', player1Cards, this.player1Div)
    this.player2 = new Player('Player 2', player2Cards, this.player2Div)
    this.player1.play()
}
```

Now, we need to make a Boolean property called `turn` in the `Player` class. When the player is created, we will set the property to `false`. When we call `play`, we will set that property to `true` so we know that the player can play:

In *player.js*:

```
/**
 * A player has the following properties
 * @param {String} name
 * @param {Array<PokemonCard>} cards
 * @param {HTMLDivElement} div The div to show the cards in
 */
constructor(name, cards, div) {
    this.name = name
    this.cards = cards
    this.score = 0
    this.turn = false
    this.showcards(div)
}

/**
```

```
 * The player should now take a turn
 */
play() {
    this.turn = true
}
```

A player should only be able to click on their cards, when it is their turn. So, if a player clicks on a card when it is not their turn, we should not allow that. How will we do that? Our click event handler is in the `PokemonCard` class and that doesn't know which player's turn it is or even which player the card belongs to.

To solve this problem, we need to let the card know what player it belongs to. There are many ways to do this. We can move all the card creation code into the `Player` class and pass the player to the `PokemonCard` class in the `constructor`. Or if we don't want to make that change, we can find what method in the `PokemonCard` class is called by the player and just use that. Currently when a player is created, we call `showcards`, which in turn calls the `show` method in the `PokemonCard` class. We can pass the player to the `PokemonCard` class when we call `show`:

In *PokemonCard.js*:

At the top of the file:

```
import Player from './player.js'
```

In the `show` method, we add a `player` parameter. We also check if it is not the player's turn and return out of the click handler function `showImage`:

```
/**
 * Show the image of this card in the div.
 * @param {HTMLDivElement} div
 * @param {Player} player
 */
show(div, player) {
    // create the image element
    let image = document.createElement('img')
    image.classList.add('cardImage')

    // set the src property to the back of the card
    image.src = 'https://github.com/sgd2z/elementary-
javascript/blob/master/Chapter22/images/pokemon_card_back.jpg?raw=true'

    // put the image element in the div
```

154

```
        div.appendChild(image)

        const showImage = () => {
            // Don't do anything if it is not the player's turn
            if (player.turn === false) {
                return
            }
            image.removeEventListener('click', showImage)
            image.src = this.image
        }

        // add click listener
        image.addEventListener('click', showImage)
    }
```

In *player.js*:

```
/**
 * Show all the cards in the div
 * @param {HTMLDivElement} div
 */
showcards(div) {
    let position = 0
    while (position < this.cards.length) {
        let card = this.cards[position]
        card.show(div, this)
        position = position + 1
    }
}
```

When the game starts, it is player 1's turn. Let's see if now we can only click cards for player 1:

Yay, that worked! I can only click cards for Player 1.

What should happen when Player 1 takes a turn? After Player 1 clicks on an image, its turn should end. When that happens, it needs to let the game know that the turn has ended and what card was chosen.

We have a similar problem as before; the player object doesn't know anything about the game. Let's make sure the player object knows about the game first:

In *player.js:*

```
/**
 * A player has the following properties
 * @param {String} name
 * @param {Array<PokemonCard>} cards
 * @param {HTMLDivElement} div The div to show the cards in
 * @param {Game} game
 */
constructor(name, cards, div, game) {
    this.name = name
    this.cards = cards
    this.score = 0
    this.turn = false
    this.game = game
```

```
        this.showcards(div)
    }
```

In *game.js*:

```
/**
 * Start the game.
 * Get cards, create players.
 */
async start() {
    let player1Cards = await PokemonAPI.getRandomPokemonCards(9)
    let player2Cards = await PokemonAPI.getRandomPokemonCards(9)
    this.player1 = new Player('Player 1', player1Cards, this.player1Div, this)
    this.player2 = new Player('Player 2', player2Cards, this.player2Div, this)
    this.player1.play()
}
```

Now that the player knows about the game, let's see how to end the player's turn. When the user clicks on a card, we will call an `endTurn` method in the `Player` class that we will make. In the `PokemonCard` class:

```
/**
 * Show the image of this card in the div.
 * @param {HTMLDivElement} div
 * @param {Player} player
 */
show(div, player) {
    // create the image element
    let image = document.createElement('img')
    image.classList.add('cardImage')

    // set the src property to the back of the card
    image.src = 'https://github.com/sgd2z/elementary-
javascript/blob/master/Chapter22/images/pokemon_card_back.jpg?raw=true'

    // put the image element in the div
    div.appendChild(image)

    const showImage = () => {
        // Don't do anything if it is not the player's turn
        if (player.turn === false) {
            return
        }
        image.removeEventListener('click', showImage)
        image.src = this.image
```

```
            player.endTurn(this)
        }

        // add click listener
        image.addEventListener('click', showImage)
    }
```

In the `Player` class:

```
/**
 * End the player's turn
 * @param {PokemonCard} card
 */
endTurn(card) {
    this.turn = false
    this.game.endTurn(card)
}
```

In *game.js*:

At the top of the file:

```
import PokemonCard from './pokemonCard.js'
```

In the `Game` class:

```
/**
 * End a player's turn
 * @param {PokemonCard} card
 */
endTurn(card) {

}
```

What should we do in the game's `endTurn` method? This method doesn't know who called it. We are not keeping track of whose turn it is in the game. Now we can either send back which player it was that called `endTurn` or we can just keep track of whose turn it is in the game too. Let's do that. We will add a turn property to the game and if it is Player 1's turn we will set it to 1 and if it is Player 2's turn, we will set it to 2. In *game.js*:

```
/**
 * Start the game.
 * Get cards, create players.
 */
async start() {
```

```
        let player1Cards = await PokemonAPI.getRandomPokemonCards(9)
        let player2Cards = await PokemonAPI.getRandomPokemonCards(9)
        this.player1 = new Player('Player 1', player1Cards, this.player1Div, this)
        this.player2 = new Player('Player 2', player2Cards, this.player2Div, this)
        this.turn = 1
        this.player1.play()
    }
```

Now in `endTurn` in Game we can see which card was played by which player and we can give the next player their turn:

```
    /**
     * End a player's turn
     * @param {PokemonCard} card
     */
    endTurn(card) {
        // If it is Player 1's turn, set Player1's card to "card" and give Player 2 their
turn
        if (this.turn == 1) {
            this.player1Card = card
            this.turn = 2
            this.player2.play()
        } else { // Otherwise it is Player 2's turn, set Player 2's card to "card" and
give Player 1 their turn
            this.player2Card = card
            this.turn = 1
            this.player1.play()
        }
    }
```

Now let's see if all this works and the players get their turns alternately:

It worked!! I had to click on a card for Player 1, then on one for Player 2. Nothing happened when I click on Player 1's cards when it was not Player 1's turn or Player 2's card when it was not Player 2's turn.

Attacks

Next thing we need to do is figure out how to attack! Once both players have chosen cards, we need the Pokémon's to attack each other. Let's see how we can make attacks happen. The rules we made up for the game said that we need to choose an attack randomly. Let's make an attack method to PokemonCard and it will select an attack randomly for us for the card. In *pokemonCard.js*:

```
/**
 * Return a random attack for this card
 */
attack() {
    let randomIndex = Math.floor(Math.random() * this.attacks.length)
    return this.attacks[randomIndex]
}
```

Now in the game, when both players have chosen cards, we will attack. How do we know both players have chosen cards? In the `endTurn` method after each player's turn, we will check and then call a new method called `fight`. In *game.js*:

```
/**
 * The Pokemon attack each other
 */
fight() {

}

/**
 * End a player's turn
 * @param {PokemonCard} card
 */
endTurn(card) {
    // If it is Player 1's turn, set Player1's card to "card" and give Player 2 their
turn
    if (this.turn == 1) {
        this.player1Card = card
        if (this.player2Card !== undefined) {
            this.fight()
        }
        this.turn = 2
        this.player2.play()
    } else { // Otherwise it is Player 2's turn, set Player 2's card to "card" and
give Player 1 their turn
        this.player2Card = card
        if (this.player1Card !== undefined) {
            this.fight()
        }
        this.turn = 1
        this.player1.play()
    }
}
```

Now, just like we keep track of whose turn it is for selecting a card, we will keep track of who is attacking. In *game.js*:

```
/**
 * Start the game.
 * Get cards, create players.
 */
async start() {
```

```
    let player1Cards = await PokemonAPI.getRandomPokemonCards(9)
    let player2Cards = await PokemonAPI.getRandomPokemonCards(9)
    this.player1 = new Player('Player 1', player1Cards, this.player1Div, this)
    this.player2 = new Player('Player 2', player2Cards, this.player2Div, this)
    this.turn = 1
    this.attacker = 1
    this.player1.play()
}
```

In the `fight` method:

```
/**
 * The Pokemon attack each other
 */
fight() {
    if (this.attacker === 1) {
        let attack = this.player1Card.attack()
    } else if (this.attacker === 2) {
        let attack = this.player2Card.attack()
    }
}
```

Notice that we are never changing the attacker from Player 1 to Player 2. Once we have an attack, we need to damage the other player's card by the amount of the attack. For that let's make a `damage` method on the `PokemonCard` class. When we call `damage`, we will reduce the `HP` of the card by the amount of the damage.

```
/**
 * get Attacked.
 * @param {Number} attackDamage
 */
damage(attackDamage) {
    this.HP = this.HP - attackDamage
}
```

Let's update the `fight` method to do this and to change the attacker each time:

```
/**
 * The Pokemon attack each other
 */
fight() {
    if (this.attacker === 1) {
        let attack = this.player1Card.attack()
        this.player2Card.damage(attack.damage)
        this.attacker = 2
    } else if (this.attacker === 2) {
```

```
        let attack = this.player2Card.attack()
        this.player1Card.damage(attack.damage)
        this.attacker = 1
    }
}
```

The next thing we need to do is check if the HP of a PokemonCard became 0 or less. If that happens, that card is out of the game and the player gets to choose a card. We must do many things to make this happen:

- After each attack check if the HP are less than or equal to 0

- If they are, then that player gets a turn. This means that we need to change our turn logic in endTurn and move it to the fight method

- If the HP are not less than or equal to zero, then the other PokemonCard attacks. So, we need to call the fight method again.

Let's see how this would work in the fight method:

```
/**
 * The Pokemon attack each other
 */
fight() {
    if (this.attacker === 1) {
        let attack = this.player1Card.attack()
        this.player2Card.damage(attack.damage)
        this.attacker = 2
// If player 2's card is defeated
        if (this.player2Card.HP <= 0) {
            this.turn = 2
            this.player2.play()
        } else {
            this.fight()
        }
    } else if (this.attacker === 2) {
        let attack = this.player2Card.attack()
        this.player1Card.damage(attack.damage)
        this.attacker = 1
// If player 1's card is defeated
        if (this.player1Card.HP <= 0) {
            this.turn = 1
            this.player1.play()
```

163

```
        } else {
            this.fight()
        }
    }
}
```

Now that the `fight` method controls whose turn it is, let's change the turn logic in the `endTurn` method in `Game` to only happen if the other player does not have a card:

```
/**
 * End a player's turn
 * @param {PokemonCard} card
 */
endTurn(card) {
    // If it is Player 1's turn, set Player1's card to "card" and give Player 2 their turn
    if (this.turn == 1) {
        this.player1Card = card
        if (this.player2Card !== undefined) {
            this.fight()
        } else {
            this.turn = 2
            this.player2.play()
        }
    } else { // Otherwise it is Player 2's turn, set Player 2's card to "card" and give Player 1 their turn
        this.player2Card = card
        if (this.player1Card !== undefined) {
            this.fight()
        } else {
            this.turn = 1
            this.player1.play()
        }
    }
}
```

Let's try this out. After clicking around for some time, it looks like the game is behaving strangely. Sometimes it gets stuck at Player 1 or Player 2 always having a turn. Also, we have no idea what is going on or whose turn it is.

At this point we have two options, debug while playing to figure out what the problem is or continue and show on the screen whose turn it is, how many hit points are remaining, move the cards that are attacking to the arena and just naturally discover the problem because the information will be available on the screen.

Let's choose option 2.

Displaying Game Information

On the left is a wireframe for the battle arena `div`. We'll show game information at the top and in the middle, we'll show the cards that are played.

Let's add `div`s for this. We'll add one `div` for the game information. One `div` that contains both the player cards.

Note that Player 1's card always comes first and Player 2's card always comes second. We will learn how to set styles using JavaScript for that.

Then we'll put both those `div`s in the battle arena `div`.

In *game.js*:

```
/**
 * Setup all the things we need for the game
 */
constructor() {
    // create the divs for the players and the battle arena
    this.player1Div = document.createElement('div')
    this.player1Div.id = "player1div"

    this.player2Div = document.createElement('div')
    this.player2Div.id = "player2div"

    this.battleArena = document.createElement('div')
    this.battleArena.id = "battleArena"

    this.gameInformationDiv = document.createElement('div')
    this.gameInformationDiv.id = "gameInformationDiv"
    this.battleArena.appendChild(this.gameInformationDiv)
```

```
        this.playerCardsDiv = document.createElement('div')
        this.playerCardsDiv.id = "playerCardsDiv"
        this.battleArena.appendChild(this.playerCardsDiv)

        // create the main container div
        let mainDiv = document.createElement('div')
        mainDiv.id = "maindiv"

        // add the player and the battle arena divs to the the main div
        mainDiv.appendChild(this.player1Div)
        mainDiv.appendChild(this.battleArena)
        mainDiv.appendChild(this.player2Div)

        // show the main div
        document.body.appendChild(mainDiv)
    }
```

Next, when a player clicks a card, we'll move the card image to the `playerCardsDiv` div. To make this happen, we need to know what the HTML image element of the card is. We currently only have that as a variable in the `show` method of `PokemonCard`. Let's make that a property of the `PokemonCard` object:

```
    /**
     * Show the image of this card in the div.
     * @param {HTMLDivElement} div
     * @param {Player} player
     */
    show(div, player) {
        // create the image element
        let image = document.createElement('img')
        this.imageElement = image // we are calling this imageElement so that we don't
overwrite this.image, which contains the URL of the image.
        image.classList.add('cardImage')

        // set the src property to the back of the card
        image.src = 'https://github.com/sgd2z/elementary-
javascript/blob/master/Chapter22/images/pokemon_card_back.jpg?raw=true'

        // put the image element in the div
        div.appendChild(image)

        const showImage = () => {
            // Don't do anything if it is not the player's turn
            if (player.turn === false) {
```

```
                    return
                }
            image.removeEventListener('click', showImage)
            image.src = this.image
            player.endTurn(this)
        }

        // add click listener
        image.addEventListener('click', showImage)
    }
```

Next, when the player calls endTurn, we can move the image element to the playerCardsDiv. In endTurn in *game.js*:

```
    /**
     * End a player's turn
     * @param {PokemonCard} card
     */
    endTurn(card) {
        // If it is Player 1's turn, set Player1's card to "card" and give Player 2 their
turn
        if (this.turn == 1) {
            // move the card image to the playerCardsDiv
            this.playerCardsDiv.appendChild(card.imageElement)
            // set order = 1 so it comes first
            card.imageElement.style.order = 1
            this.player1Card = card
            if (this.player2Card !== undefined) {
                this.fight()
            } else {
                this.turn = 2
                this.player2.play()
            }
        } else { // Otherwise it is Player 2's turn, set Player 2's card to "card" and
give Player 1 their turn
            // move the card image to the playerCardsDiv
            this.playerCardsDiv.appendChild(card.imageElement)
            // set order = 2 so it comes second
            card.imageElement.style.order = 2
            this.player2Card = card
            if (this.player1Card !== undefined) {
                this.fight()
            } else {
                this.turn = 1
```

```
            this.player1.play()
        }
    }
}
```

In the above code, look at how we changed the style of the element: `card.imageElement.style.order = 1`. For the `order` style to work, we need to set the style of the parent to Flexbox. Add this to your *styles.css*:

```
#playerCardsDiv {
    display: flex
}
```

Let's see if this worked:

The card sizes look too small. Let's think about this a little. We styled our cards to fit in the `div`s where all the cards are shown. Maybe we should just remove the `cardImage` CSS class from the cards and then decide if we want to add another class to them to style them differently when they are in the `playerCardsDiv`. Just like we have the `classList.add` method, we have a `classList.remove` method to remove CSS classes. In *game.js* in `endTurn`:

```
    /**
     * End a player's turn
     * @param {PokemonCard} card
     */
    endTurn(card) {
        // If it is Player 1's turn, set Player1's card to "card" and give Player 2 their
turn
        if (this.turn == 1) {
            // remove the cardImage CSS class from the card
            card.imageElement.classList.remove('cardImage')
            // move the card image to the playerCardsDiv
            this.playerCardsDiv.appendChild(card.imageElement)
            // set order = 1 so it comes first
            card.imageElement.style.order = 1
            this.player1Card = card
            if (this.player2Card !== undefined) {
                this.fight()
            } else {
                this.turn = 2
                this.player2.play()
            }
        } else { // Otherwise it is Player 2's turn, set Player 2's card to "card" and
give Player 1 their turn
            // remove the cardImage CSS class from the card
            card.imageElement.classList.remove('cardImage')
            // move the card image to the playerCardsDiv
            this.playerCardsDiv.appendChild(card.imageElement)
            // set order = 2 so it comes second
            card.imageElement.style.order = 2
            this.player2Card = card
            if (this.player1Card !== undefined) {
                this.fight()
            } else {
                this.turn = 1
                this.player1.play()
            }
        }
    }
}
```

Let's see how that looks:

Now the cards are too big. The maximum width of those images should not be more than 50%. Let's add a new CSS class to the images when they are in the `playerCardsDiv`:

```
    /**
     * End a player's turn
     * @param {PokemonCard} card
     */
    endTurn(card) {
        // If it is Player 1's turn, set Player1's card to "card" and give Player 2 their
turn
        if (this.turn == 1) {
            // remove the cardImage CSS class from the card
            card.imageElement.classList.remove('cardImage')
            card.imageElement.classList.add('cardImageWhileAttacking')
            // move the card image to the playerCardsDiv
            this.playerCardsDiv.appendChild(card.imageElement)
            // set order = 1 so it comes first
            card.imageElement.style.order = 1
            this.player1Card = card
            if (this.player2Card !== undefined) {
```

```
                this.fight()
            } else {
                this.turn = 2
                this.player2.play()
            }
        } else { // Otherwise it is Player 2's turn, set Player 2's card to "card" and
give Player 1 their turn
            // remove the cardImage CSS class from the card
            card.imageElement.classList.remove('cardImage')
            card.imageElement.classList.add('cardImageWhileAttacking')
            // move the card image to the playerCardsDiv
            this.playerCardsDiv.appendChild(card.imageElement)
            // set order = 2 so it comes second
            card.imageElement.style.order = 2
            this.player2Card = card
            if (this.player1Card !== undefined) {
                this.fight()
            } else {
                this.turn = 1
                this.player1.play()
            }
        }
    }
}
```

Let's add styles for this class:

```
.cardImageWhileAttacking {
    max-width: 50%;
}
```

Let's see what that got us:

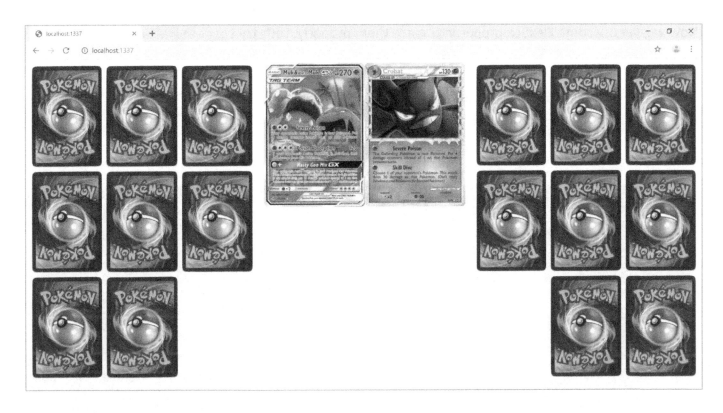

Much better. But still too big. Let's try `40%` as the `max-width`:

Now we can use some Flexbox property to space them properly. Let's try `space-between`:

```
#playerCardsDiv {
    display: flex;
    justify-content: space-between
}
```

That looks neat. You can try `space-around`, `space-evenly` and see how they work and choose the one you like best.

Let's keep clicking and see what happens:

It doesn't work too well. Sometimes clicks just stop working or sometimes you can click, and the cards just keep piling on.

Before we try to fix that, let's show whose turn it is in the game information `div` - `gameInformationDiv`. Looking at the code, it looks like we change turns in many places – look for "`this.turn =`". Instead of adding code everywhere to show whose turn it is, let's just make a method for that. Also, this is not the only information we will be showing, so let's make a `div` to show whose turn it is and then use the function to show that in the `div`.

In the `constructor` for Game:

```
/**
 * Setup all the things we need for the game
 */
constructor() {
    // create the divs for the players and the battle arena
    this.player1Div = document.createElement('div')
    this.player1Div.id = "player1div"

    this.player2Div = document.createElement('div')
    this.player2Div.id = "player2div"
```

```
    this.battleArena = document.createElement('div')
    this.battleArena.id = "battleArena"

    this.gameInformationDiv = document.createElement('div')
    this.gameInformationDiv.id = "gameInformationDiv"
    this.battleArena.appendChild(this.gameInformationDiv)

    this.turnDiv = document.createElement('div')
    this.turnDiv.id = "turnDiv"
    this.gameInformationDiv.appendChild(this.turnDiv)

    this.playerCardsDiv = document.createElement('div')
    this.playerCardsDiv.id = "playerCardsDiv"
    this.battleArena.appendChild(this.playerCardsDiv)

    // create the main container div
    let mainDiv = document.createElement('div')
    mainDiv.id = "maindiv"

    // add the player and the battle arena divs to the the main div
    mainDiv.appendChild(this.player1Div)
    mainDiv.appendChild(this.battleArena)
    mainDiv.appendChild(this.player2Div)

    // show the main div
    document.body.appendChild(mainDiv)
}
```

The setTurn method in Game:

```
/**
 * set turn and show whose turn it is
 * @param {Number} playerNumber
 */
setTurn(playerNumber) {
    this.turn = playerNumber
    this.turnDiv.innerHTML = 'Player ' + playerNumber + "'s turn"
}
```

Now, wherever you see this.turn = 1, change that to this.setTurn(1) and wherever you see this.turn = 2, change that to this.setTurn(2). You will have to change this in 5 places in game.js. Make sure you get all of them.

```
/**
 * Start the game.
 * Get cards, create players.
 */
async start() {
    let player1Cards = await PokemonAPI.getRandomPokemonCards(9)
    let player2Cards = await PokemonAPI.getRandomPokemonCards(9)
    this.player1 = new Player('Player 1', player1Cards, this.player1Div, this)
    this.player2 = new Player('Player 2', player2Cards, this.player2Div, this)
    this.setTurn(1)
    this.attacker = 1
    this.player1.play()
}


/**
 * The Pokemon attack each other
 */
fight() {
    if (this.attacker === 1) {
        let attack = this.player1Card.attack()
        this.player2Card.damage(attack.damage)
        this.attacker = 2
        // If player 2's card is defeated
        if (this.player2Card.HP <= 0) {
            this.setTurn(2)
            this.player2.play()
        } else {
            this.fight()
        }
    } else if (this.attacker === 2) {
        let attack = this.player2Card.attack()
        this.player1Card.damage(attack.damage)
        this.attacker = 1
        // If player 1's card is defeated
        if (this.player1Card.HP <= 0) {
            this.setTurn(1)
            this.player1.play()
        } else {
            this.fight()
        }
    }
}
```

176

```
/**
 * End a player's turn
 * @param {PokemonCard} card
 */
endTurn(card) {
    // If it is Player 1's turn, set Player1's card to "card" and give Player 2 their
turn
    if (this.turn == 1) {
        // remove the cardImage CSS class from the card
        card.imageElement.classList.remove('cardImage')
        card.imageElement.classList.add('cardImageWhileAttacking')
        // move the card image to the playerCardsDiv
        this.playerCardsDiv.appendChild(card.imageElement)
        // set order = 1 so it comes first
        card.imageElement.style.order = 1
        this.player1Card = card
        if (this.player2Card !== undefined) {
            this.fight()
        } else {
            this.setTurn(2)
            this.player2.play()
        }
    } else { // Otherwise it is Player 2's turn, set Player 2's card to "card" and
give Player 1 their turn
        // remove the cardImage CSS class from the card
        card.imageElement.classList.remove('cardImage')
        card.imageElement.classList.add('cardImageWhileAttacking')
        // move the card image to the playerCardsDiv
        this.playerCardsDiv.appendChild(card.imageElement)
        // set order = 2 so it comes second
        card.imageElement.style.order = 2
        this.player2Card = card
        if (this.player1Card !== undefined) {
            this.fight()
        } else {
            this.setTurn(1)
            this.player1.play()
        }
    }
}
```

Let's see if this works:

That works. It doesn't look very nice. Let's fix that. Google has a great set of fonts that you can use for free at - https://fonts.google.com/ - I chose this font:

https://fonts.google.com/specimen/Permanent+Marker

You can choose whichever one you like. Click on the "Select this font" at the top. Then click on the little black bar at the bottom and you should see all the code you need to use the font:

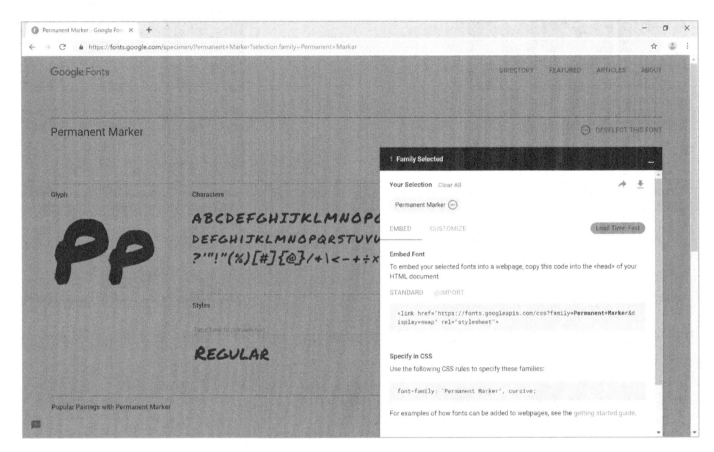

We will copy the HTML that starts with "<link" into our html file:

```
<html>
    <head>
        <link href="https://fonts.googleapis.com/css?family=Permanent+Marker&display=swap"
rel="stylesheet"></link>
        <link rel="stylesheet" href="styles.css"></link>
    </head>
    <body>
        <script src="game.js" type="module"></script>
    </body>
</html>
```

Then we can use the font-family in CSS like it says on the page and adjust the size and alignment:

```
#turnDiv {
    font-size: 25px;
    text-align: center;
```

```
    font-family: 'Permanent Marker', cursive;
}
```

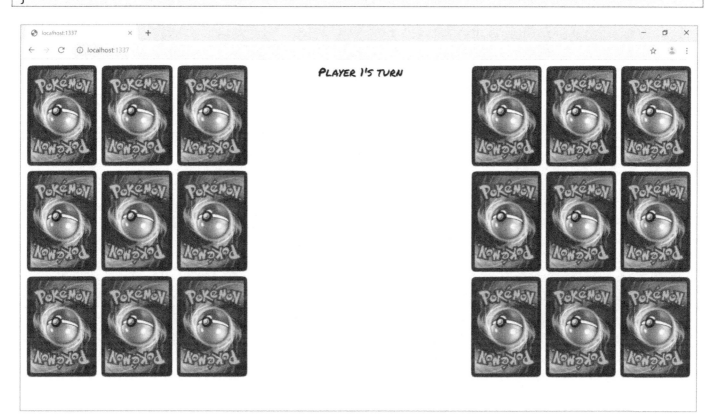

That looks nice!

Back to Attacks

Now that we have some information on whose turn it is, let's start displaying who is attacking and what attack is chosen. Let's create an attackDiv in the Game constructor to show that:

```
/**
 * Setup all the things we need for the game
 */
constructor() {
    // create the divs for the players and the battle arena
    this.player1Div = document.createElement('div')
```

```
    this.player1Div.id = "player1div"

    this.player2Div = document.createElement('div')
    this.player2Div.id = "player2div"

    this.battleArena = document.createElement('div')
    this.battleArena.id = "battleArena"

    this.gameInformationDiv = document.createElement('div')
    this.gameInformationDiv.id = "gameInformationDiv"
    this.battleArena.appendChild(this.gameInformationDiv)

    this.turnDiv = document.createElement('div')
    this.turnDiv.id = "turnDiv"
    this.gameInformationDiv.appendChild(this.turnDiv)

    this.attackDiv = document.createElement('div')
    this.attackDiv.id = "turnDiv"
    this.gameInformationDiv.appendChild(this.attackDiv)

    this.playerCardsDiv = document.createElement('div')
    this.playerCardsDiv.id = "playerCardsDiv"
    this.battleArena.appendChild(this.playerCardsDiv)

    // create the main container div
    let mainDiv = document.createElement('div')
    mainDiv.id = "maindiv"

    // add the player and the battle arena divs to the the main div
    mainDiv.appendChild(this.player1Div)
    mainDiv.appendChild(this.battleArena)
    mainDiv.appendChild(this.player2Div)

    // show the main div
    document.body.appendChild(mainDiv)
}
```

Next, we'll show attack information using a new method in the `Game class` called `showAttackInfo` that shows which player, which card and which attack were chosen and the attack damage:

```
/**
 * Show who is attacking and what the attack is
 * @param {Player} player
 * @param {PokemonCard} card
```

```
 * @param {*} attack
 */
showAttackInfo(playerNumber, card, attack) {
    this.attackDiv.innerHTML = 'Player ' + playerNumber + "'s " + card.name + ' is
attacking with ' + attack.name + ". Damage is " + attack.damage
}
```

Now, every time we attack, we will call this method:

```
/**
 * The Pokemon attack each other
 */
    fight() {
        if (this.attacker === 1) {
            let attack = this.player1Card.attack()
            this.showAttackInfo(1, this.player1Card, attack)
            this.player2Card.damage(attack.damage)
            this.attacker = 2
            // If player 2's card is defeated
            if (this.player2Card.HP <= 0) {
                this.setTurn(2)
                this.player2.play()
            } else {
                this.fight()
            }
        } else if (this.attacker === 2) {
            let attack = this.player2Card.attack()
            this.showAttackInfo(2, this.player2Card, attack)
            this.player1Card.damage(attack.damage)
            this.attacker = 1
            // If player 1's card is defeated
            if (this.player1Card.HP <= 0) {
                this.setTurn(1)
                this.player1.play()
            } else {
                this.fight()
            }
        }
    }
}
```

Here is what happens when we do that:

It directly shows us Player 2's attack. It should have shown us Player 1's attack. But things happen too fast for us to see. So, let's slow things down a bit.

Slowing Things Down

This is where all the things we learned in Chapter 21 with waits and timers will come in handy. Let's make a new file called *helper.js* and make a helper object in it where we will put the `numberOfSeconds` function.

In *helper.js*:

```
const Helper = {
    numberOfSeconds: (secondsToWait) => {
        /**
         * @param {Function} keepPromise When this function is called, Javascript know
that you finished doing what you promised
         */
        let promiser = (keepPromise) => {
            /**
             * This function is the one that is called after waiting the number of seconds
required
             */
```

```
        let functionToCallAfterSeconds = () => {
            // We are done waiting so we finished doing what we promised.
            keepPromise()
        }
        // Wait for secondsToWait and call functionToCallAfterSeconds
        setTimeout(functionToCallAfterSeconds, secondsToWait * 1000)
    }

    // Create a promise object and return it. This turns this function into an async
function
    let promise = new Promise(promiser)
    return promise
    }
  }
}

export default Helper
```

Now let's wait for a couple of seconds after each attack. In *game.js*:

At the top:

```
import Helper from './helper.js'
```

We will convert the `fight` method to `async` so that we can use `await` in it to wait for two seconds. Also, we need to `await` the call to `fight` itself because we need to wait for that to finish before the next attack. Now that our `fight` method is getting big, we also might want to add more comments so that the code stays readable. The new comments for old code are not highlighted. In the `fight` method:

```
/**
 * The Pokemon attack each other
 */
async fight() {
    if (this.attacker === 1) {
        // get the attack that Player 1's card makes
        let attack = this.player1Card.attack()
        this.showAttackInfo(1, this.player1Card, attack)
        await Helper.numberOfSeconds(2)
        // attack player 2's card:
        this.player2Card.damage(attack.damage)
        // now it is player 2's turn to attack
        this.attacker = 2
        // If player 2's card is defeated
        if (this.player2Card.HP <= 0) {
            // remove the defeated card
```

```
                    this.player2
                  · // it is player 2's turn
                    this.setTurn(2)
                    this.player2.play()
                } else {
                    await this.fight()
                }
            } else if (this.attacker === 2) {
                let attack = this.player2Card.attack()
                this.showAttackInfo(2, this.player2Card, attack)
                await Helper.numberOfSeconds(2)
                this.player1Card.damage(attack.damage)
                this.attacker = 1
                // If player 1's card is defeated
                if (this.player1Card.HP <= 0) {
                    this.setTurn(1)
                    this.player1.play()
                } else {
                    await this.fight()
                }
            }
        }
    }
}
```

Now let's see if we can see Player 1's attack and then Player 2's attack. Yes! We do see Player 1's and Player2's attacks happening one after another. But it is confusing to always see someone's turn being shown while the attacks are happening. Let's hide whose turn it is while attacks are happening. That is easy. Just do this in the first line of the `fight` method:

```
this.turnDiv.innerHTML = ""
```

The next confusing thing is that even when all the attacking is done and it is the next player's turn, we can still see the last attack. Let's remove the attack by emptying the `attackDiv` once all the attacking is done and the next player needs to take a turn. Where do you think we should do that? I did it in the `setTurn` method:

```
/**
 * set turn and show whose turn it is
 * @param {Number} playerNumber
 */
setTurn(playerNumber) {
    this.turn = playerNumber
    this.attackDiv.innerHTML = ""
    this.turnDiv.innerHTML = 'Player ' + playerNumber + "'s turn"
```

```
    }
```

Much better. Now the Pokémon are attacking alternately, and we get to the next person's turn. Let's continue playing. Ah, the two cards stay on the screen and a third one shows up:

We now need to figure out how to remove the defeated card from the player's list of cards and from the arena. We can do that when the HP of the Pokémon card goes to zero or less. We can do this in the game while attacking or we can do this in the `damage` method of `PokemonCard`. Let's do this in the `damage` method. However, in the `damage` method of `PokemonCard`, we do not know who the player is. Is there any method in the `PokemonCard` class where we get the player? Yes, we do - in the `show` method of `PokemonCard`. To use that in other methods, we can make that a property of the object when we get it.

This is how we do it. In the `show` method of `PokemonCard`:

```
/**
 * Show the image of this card in the div.
 * @param {HTMLDivElement} div
 * @param {Player} player
 */
show(div, player) {
    // save the player for later use
    this.player = player
```

```
    // create the image element
    let image = document.createElement('img')
    this.imageElement = image // we are calling this imageElement so that we don't
overwrite "this.image", which contains the URL of the image.
    image.classList.add('cardImage')

    // set the src property to the back of the card
    image.src = 'https://github.com/sgd2z/elementary-
javascript/blob/master/Chapter22/images/pokemon_card_back.jpg?raw=true'

    // put the image element in the div
    div.appendChild(image)

    const showImage = () => {
        // Don't do anything if it is not the player's turn
        if (player.turn === false) {
            return
        }
        image.removeEventListener('click', showImage)
        image.src = this.image
        player.endTurn(this)
    }

    // add click listener
    image.addEventListener('click', showImage)
}
```

Now that we have the player as a property, in the damage method of the PokemonCard class:

```
/**
 * get Attacked.
 * @param {Number} attackDamage
 */
damage(attackDamage) {
    this.HP = this.HP - attackDamage
    // if the card is defeated, remove from the player list and delete the element
    if (this.HP <= 0) {
        // this is how you delete an HTML element. By removing it from the
parentElement
        this.imageElement.parentElement.removeChild(this.imageElement)
        this.player.removeCard(this)
    }
}
```

Look at the call to `removeCard`. We are sending it the card. However, the `removeCard` method in the `Player` class, as we have currently made it, needs the index of the card. So, our call to `removeCard` will not work. We will have to rewrite it to find the card and remove it when it is found. JavaScript's lists are great, and they have a method called `filter` that can do that but since we haven't learned about that yet, let's see if we can figure out the code ourselves.

```
/**
 * remove the card specified from the list of cards
 * @param {PokemonCard} card
 */
removeCard(card) {
    let position = 0;
    while (position < this.cards.length) {
        let cardAtPosition = this.cards[position]
        if (cardAtPosition === card) {
            this.cards.splice(position, 1)
            return
        }
        position = position + 1
    }
}
```

Let's see if this works:

This works to remove the cards when they are defeated. But often the battles keep on going forever when they clearly should end pretty fast. Look at the screenshot and see if you can tell if something is wrong and if so, what it is. If you guessed 50x is not a number, you are correct. Also, occasionally we get attacks which have no damage, like this:

So, now we must solve two problems:

- Attacks with no damage specified.

- Attacks with damage that is not a number (In JavaScript if you are debugging and do Math operations on things that are not a number, they will show up as NaN).

If we were debugging, trying to solve this problem, we could have put a breakpoint in the damage method of PokemonCard where the calculations are happening, and this is what we would have seen:

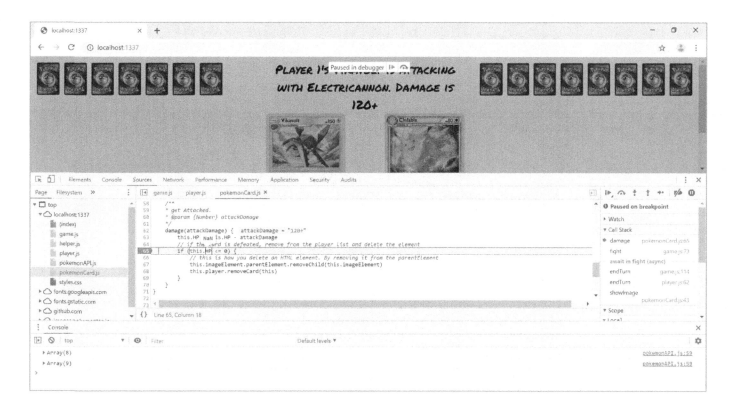

The computer doesn't know how to deal with something like 120+ or 50x, which are not numbers and something that has no damage, i.e. is not a number.

How do we deal with that? Well, when we select our Pokémon for the players how about we only select Pokémon that have attacks with damage and if we have damage that is not a number, we convert it to a number.

Can you figure out how to do that in the getRandomPokemonCards function in the PokemonAPI object? You will have to find out how to convert something into a number. Can you Google it and figure it out?

Here is one way to do it:

```
/**
 * Gets a random selection of Pokemon cards
 * @param {Number} number the number of cards to get
 */
getRandomPokemonCards: async (number) => {
    // Get cards using the API
    let pokemonList = await PokemonAPI.getPokemonList()

    // Create a list
    let pokemonCards = []
```

```
        // Create a loop to get "number" cards
        let counter = 0
        while (counter < number) {
            // select a random card
            let randomIndex = randomBetween(0, pokemonList.length)
            let pokemon = pokemonList[randomIndex]

            // create a new list of good attacks
            let goodAttacks = []

            // add all attacks where the damage can be converted to a number to good
attacks.

            let position = 0
            while (position < pokemon.attacks.length) {
                let attack = pokemon.attacks[position]
                attack.damage = parseInt(attack.damage)
                if (attack.damage > 0) {
                    goodAttacks.push(attack)
                }
                position++
            }

            // replace attacks with good attacks
            pokemon.attacks = goodAttacks

            // only use pokemon that have good attacks
            if (pokemon.attacks.length > 0) {
                // create a PokemonCard object from the card to use in the game
                let pokemonCard = new PokemonCard(pokemon.name, pokemon.hp,
pokemon.imageUrl, pokemon.attacks)

                // add the card to our list
                pokemonCards.push(pokemonCard)
                counter = counter + 1
            }
        }

        console.log(pokemonCards)
        return pokemonCards
    }
```

Can you understand what we did? We created a new list called goodAttacks and then we looped through all the attacks and only added them to goodAttacks if we could convert to a number > 0. Then we replaced the attacks of the card with only the goodAttacks. After that, we only added cards to the list of cards if they had at least 1 good attack by checking pokemon.attacks.length > 0.

Let's try the game out now! It works great. Now we can see all the attacks for two seconds and then the card that is attacked goes away when it is supposed to. Our game is now fully working – almost!!! As I kept playing, I ran into one more problem. A card with no HP like the Legend card below:

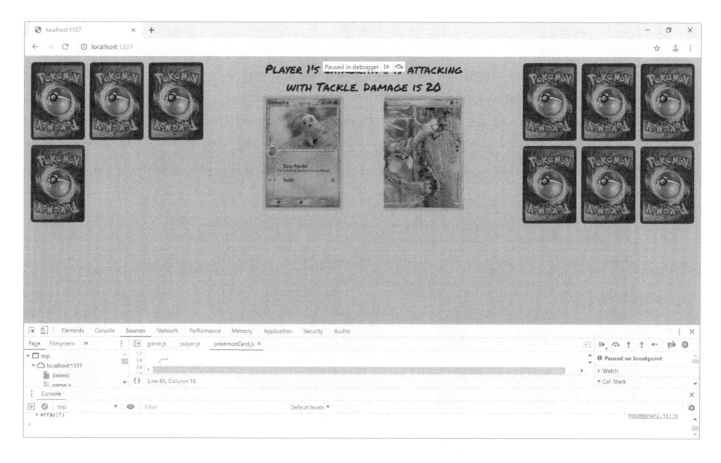

Can you figure out how to deal with that? Maybe you could do something like this:

```
if (pokemon.attacks.length > 0 && pokemon.hp > 0) {
```

Exercise

Before we finish, just know that as an exercise, I'm leaving you some little problems in the game.

- The first one is that when it is Player 1's turn, Player 2's card shows up in the spot where Player 1's card is supposed to be. Can you fix that?

- The second is that sometimes the game does not load and there is an error in the console. Refresh the page for the game a few times and see if you run into that problem. Can you put a breakpoint at the problem spot and figure out what to do?

The solution to these problems is in Chapter 24 but try and figure it out yourself.

* * *

The last thing we need to do is figure out when the game ends and who won. The game ends when all the cards for one player are defeated. One place we know that is in the removeCard function. When we remove cards from the player's cards, we can check if there are no cards remaining. If there are none, then the player loses and the game ends. Let's make an end method in the Game class that ends the game. The losing player will call that function. So, in the end method we need to know who that player is, and it will need a player parameter:

```
/**
 * End the game
 * @param {Player} player
 */
end(player) {
    if (player === this.player1) {
        this.turnDiv.innerHTML = 'Player 2 Wins!'
    } else {
        this.turnDiv.innerHTML = 'Player 1 Wins!'
    }
}
```

We will call this from removeCard in *player.js*:

```
/**
 * remove the card specified from the list of cards
 * @param {PokemonCard} card
 */
removeCard(card) {
    let position = 0;
    while (position < this.cards.length) {
        let cardAtPosition = this.cards[position]
        if (cardAtPosition === card) {
```

```
        this.cards.splice(position, 1)
        // if there are no cards left, the player loses
        if (this.cards.length === 0) {
            this.game.end(this)
        }
        return
    }
    position = position + 1
}
}
```

Now try playing the game. It looks like it never gets to end because even at the end instead of telling us `'Player 2 Wins!'` or `'Player 1 Wins!'`, it still tells us that a player needs to take a turn. Why do you think that happens? Can you debug and find out? Can you tell just by thinking of the code?

Let's try and figure it out together. Let's put a breakpoint in end to make sure we are getting there:

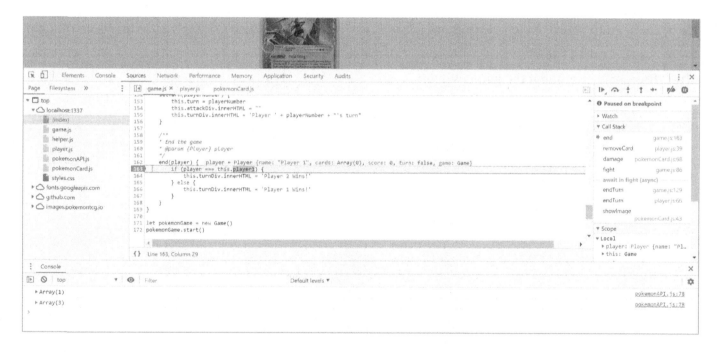

This means that we are getting to the end method, but the game keeps on going. If you think about all the code we wrote so far, that's how the code works. In our `fight` method, the turns keep on going. We never check if the game is over or if the players have run out of cards.

As always, there are many ways of doing things in code and we could have checked if a player is out of cards in the `fight` method. But now we need to check if the game is over. Let us set a `gameOver` property in the `end` method:

```
/**
 * End the game
 * @param {Player} player the player that lost
 */
end(player) {
    // The game is over!
    this.gameOver = true
    if (player === this.player1) {
        this.turnDiv.innerHTML = "Player 2 Wins!"
    } else {
        this.turnDiv.innerHTML = "Player 1 Wins!"
    }
}
```

Next, we need to figure out where to check in the `fight` method for gameOver. Let's give this some thought. removeCard is called from the `damage` method. So, the game can only end after we call damage. We will check after the `damage` method if the game is over:

```
async fight() {
    this.turnDiv.innerHTML = ""
    if (this.attacker === 1) {
        // get the attack that Player 1's card makes
        let attack = this.player1Card.attack()
        this.showAttackInfo(1, this.player1Card, attack)
        await Helper.numberOfSeconds(2)
        // attack player 2's card:
        this.player2Card.damage(attack.damage)

        // Don't continue if the game is over.
        if (this.gameOver) {
            return
        }

        // now it is player 2's turn to attack
        this.attacker = 2
        // If player 2's card is defeated:
        if (this.player2Card.HP <= 0) {
            // remove the defeated card
            this.player2
```

```
                // it is player 2's turn
                this.setTurn(2)
                this.player2.play()
            } else {
                await this.fight()
            }
        } else if (this.attacker === 2) {
            let attack = this.player2Card.attack()
            this.showAttackInfo(2, this.player2Card, attack)
            await Helper.numberOfSeconds(2)
            this.player1Card.damage(attack.damage)

            // Don't continue if the game is over.
            if (this.gameOver) {
                return
            }

            this.attacker = 1
            if (this.player1Card.HP <= 0) {
                this.setTurn(1)
                this.player1.play()
            } else {
                await this.fight()
            }
        }
    }
}
```

Let's test if that worked. It did! But we still have the last attack showing after a player wins.

196

Let's cleanup `attackDiv` when the game ends:

```
/**
 * End the game
 * @param {Player} player the player that lost
 */
end(player) {
    // The game is over!
    this.gameOver = true
    if (player === this.player1) {
        this.turnDiv.innerHTML = "Player 2 Wins!"
    } else {
        this.turnDiv.innerHTML = "Player 1 Wins!"
    }
    this.attackDiv.innerHTML = ""
}
```

There, done! Our game works now.

Exercise

Here are some more things that will make the game better:

- Can you figure out how to make the game restart after it is over?

- Can you figure out how to alternate who starts the game? First time, Player 1 starts, next time Player 2 starts and so on.

- Instead of alternate starts, can you figure out how to make the winner start in the next game?

CHAPTER 23: LETTING PEOPLE PLAY OUR GAME

Now that we have our game, we need to put it up somewhere so other people can play it. There are a lot of choices on where we can put up our game. There are 100s of small and large web hosting services. Let's quickly go through some options:

- Shared Hosting: Shared hosting is where you rent a small amount of resources on a server that is shared with a lot of other websites. Think of this as renting a room in a house.

- Virtual Private Server: This is where you have your own private server space on a server that is also shared with other people who have their own private space. Think of this as renting an apartment in an apartment building.

- Private Server: This is your own server that you do not share with others. Think of this as renting an entire house.

- Cloud: Think of the cloud as a large neighborhood where you can rent what you want when you want based on what your needs are.

Personally, I host my website on a very cheap shared hosting service at a small hosting provider called WebHostingBuzz. When I ran the Internet Book Database, I hosted using a "virtual private server" at a web host called JaguarPC. Generally, at the companies I work at, things are hosted in the cloud because we can choose to get more or less resources as we need them.

The advantage of shared hosting for something small is that it is easy to setup and somebody else does all the server management and it is very cheap. Sometimes you can host your stuff on the Internet for less than 5$/month and often shared hosts will even throw in a domain name for free!

Now let's see what we need to do to get our game online at a shared host. I recommend getting both hosting and your domain name from the same place because they will set everything up for you – otherwise you will have to follow instructions to setup your domain, which can be a little confusing. Once that is done, all we need to do is upload files.

My host runs a software called cPanel and when I login, I get a lot of options:

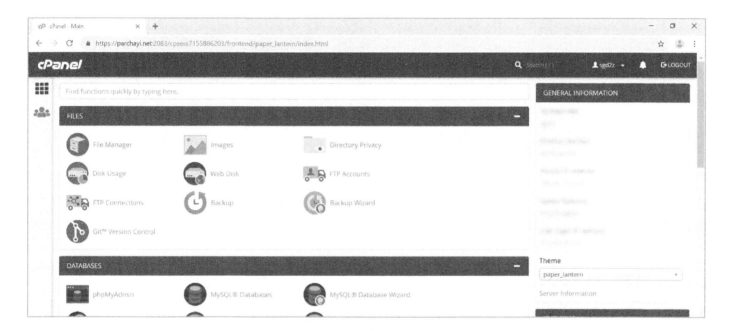

I just click on File Manager and get this:

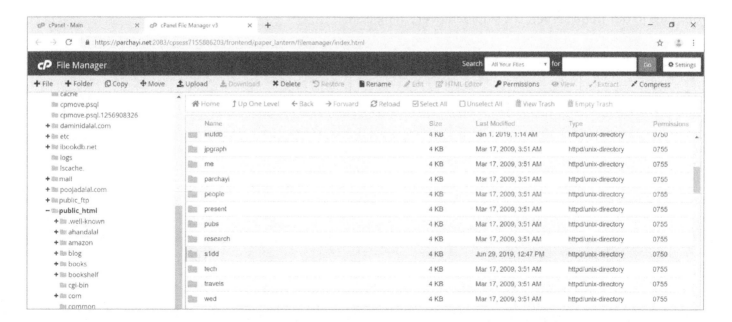

Kind of looks like the Windows File Explorer. In there, generally you need to upload to either a folder called *public_html* or a folder with your domain name. For example, my site is at https://www.s1dd.com/ and I need to upload files into a folder called *s1dd* in *public_html*. Different hosts set things up differently. Once you have the correct folder to upload things – if you don't know where, ask your host – all you need to do is click the upload button and drag and drop all the files:

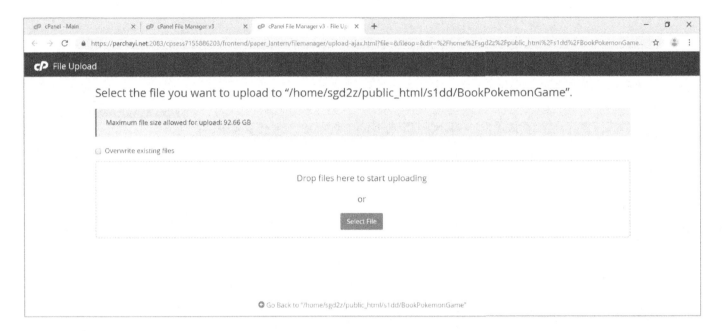

We don't need to upload our *server.js* file or the *node_modules* folder because we don't need to run our node server. The host already runs a server to serve all your files. We didn't do anything beyond just serving our files in our node server. Let's upload everything else:

Drag and drop all this stuff into your server. I've uploaded the game here:

https://s1dd.com/BookPokemonGame/

That's it. Now your game can be played by your friends online!

JavaScript can also be used to make apps for phones and tablets using a software called Cordova. JavaScript can also be used to make applications for the desktop using Electron. All of this with almost no changes to your code!

CHAPTER 24: CODING WITH FRIENDS

Writing code is a lot of work and if you are making something large and complicated you will work with your friends. In real life people work in large teams to write code. How do we make things work together? People modifying the same files, people writing different bits and pieces or solving different problems in the code and then we need to get all that work merged together. If you are not working with a friend, feel free to skip most of this chapter until you are. You might want to read on to see how we fixed the problems in the game.

For that, we use something called a Source Code Control System. A SCSS keeps track of all the versions of your code, all the history and allows multiple people to work on the same project at the same time. For the purpose of this book, we will use a product called "git" as our source code control system. In a source code control system, we store our code in a "repository", or repo in short. We will use GitHub - https://www.github.com/ - as our repository. I've even created a repository at GitHub for all the code in this book! You can find it at:

https://github.com/sgd2z/elementary-javascript

If you run into problems with any code in any of the chapters, you can always get the code from there and compare what you have with the code online.

USING GIT AND GITHUB

To use git, first we need to install git on our computer. You can download git from https://git-scm.com/. Once you have installed it on your computer, VS Code will automatically detect it and you can start using it directly from inside VS Code!

Creating a repo

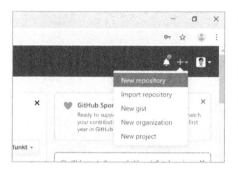

First thing you need is an account at GitHub. Once you create your account, you need to create a new repository using the button at the top right shown in the picture. This is what GitHub looks like when I wrote this book. It might change when you start working on it so you might have to find where to create a new repo from.

Cloning a repo

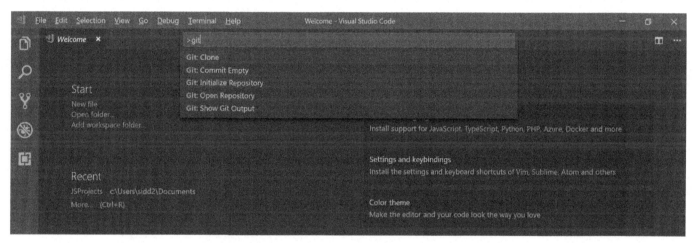

Once you have created a repository, you need to "clone" it on your computer. That is just a fancy way of saying that you will download all the code onto your computer. Inside VS Code, Press "Ctrl + Shift + P" – this is the shortcut to get to all the things you can do inside VS Code. Once you press that, type "git" in the box that shows up:

Choose "Git: Clone".

Enter the URL of the repository in the box that shows up after:

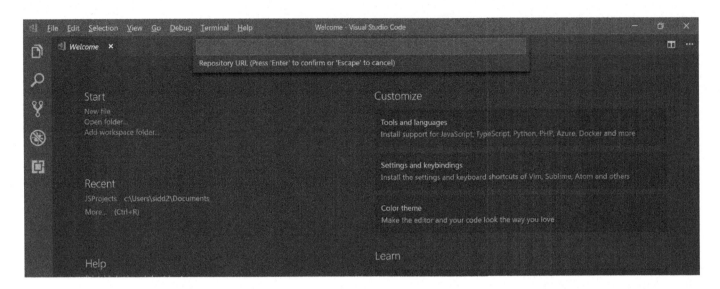

You can get the URL of the repository from GitHub from your repository. Here is the how to get it for the repo for this book by clicking the "Clone or download button":

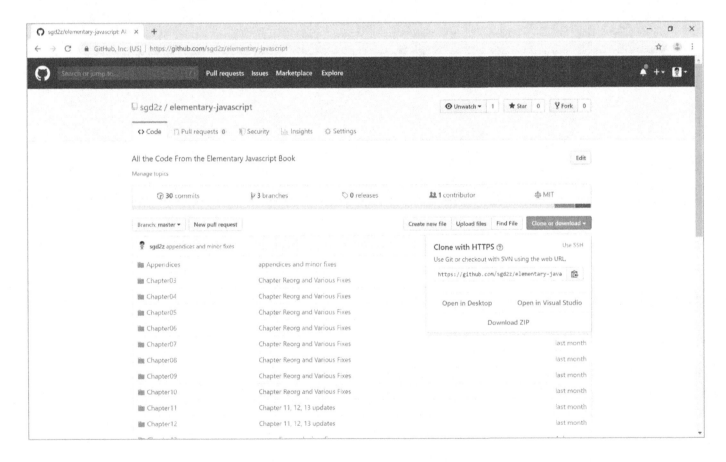

Once you clone the repository, you can open that folder in VS Code.

Remember express? The node library we installed to user our web server. We don't want to upload all that stuff to our code repository because that is a lot of files that we don't need. When you install something using npm, it automatically gets installed in a folder called *node_modules*. And to tell git to ignore that folder, we need to make a file called "*.gitignore*" in the project and put "/node_modules" in it:

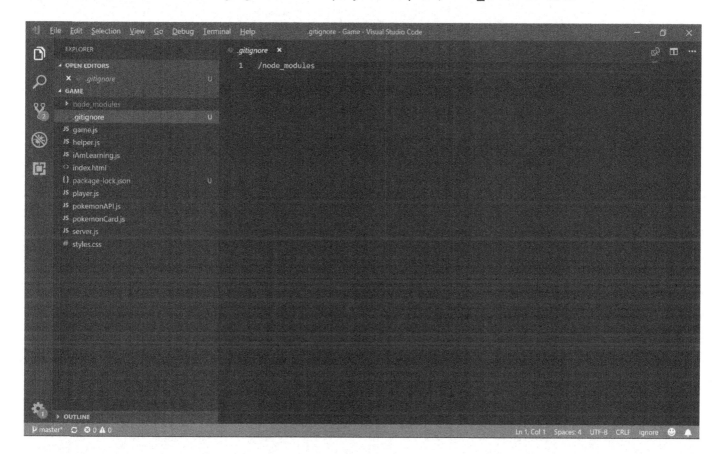

Making Changes to the Code

Let's say now when you are working on your code on your computer making changes or adding things to this repo that you cloned. What you will need to do next is save all the changes to the repo. This requires two steps, both of which you can do from inside Visual Studio Code. The first step is to commit the code. This means you are done with what you are doing and want to save all your changes.

See that button circled in red, click it. That will show you a list of files that you have changed. When you click on any of those files in the list, VS Code will show you what you have changed. For example, here is the change made to make sure we don't get cards without hit points:

Green means you added new code. Red means you removed code.

If you are happy with your changes, click the plus button next to that file. Do that for all the files. This is a good time to check to see if what you have added or removed is correct.

Then enter a message that says what change you made and click "Ctrl + Enter" to "commit" your changes. Commit only saves your changes to your computer. To put your changes online to GitHub so that other people can see them you need to "push" them. Before we push them, we need to tell VS Code the username and email of our GitHub account. Open the terminal and do this with your email and username:

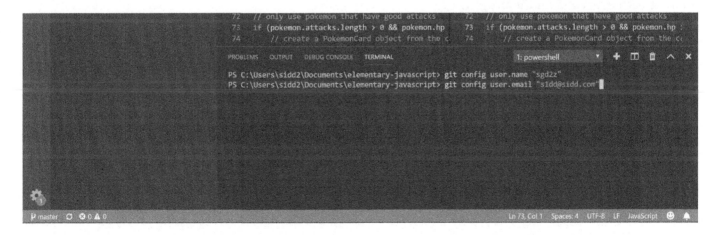

Now we are ready to push the code. To do that click the three dots and select "Push" from that menu:

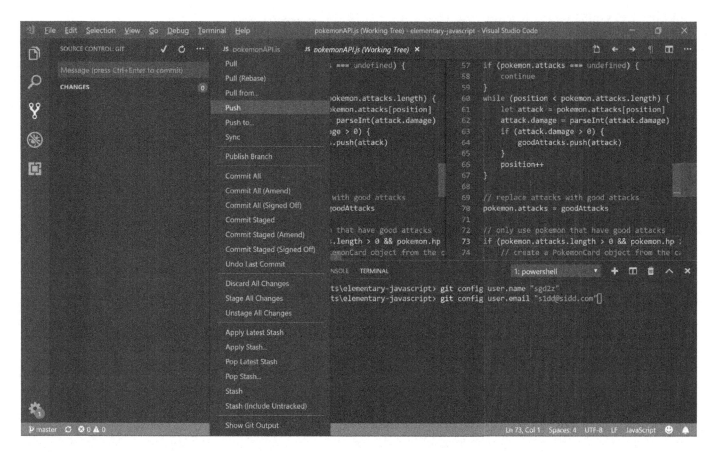

Branches

Let's say you working with many friends on a project and you are working on a new feature and don't want to mess up your working game but you still want to push your code and save it as you make progress and share it with everyone on the project.

For that you need to make a branch on the project. A branch is basically a copy of the code that is separate from the main code. By default, in GitHub, all your code is on a branch called "master". This is your main copy of the code.

Let's see how to make a branch. We'll take one of the problems we wanted to solve before. For example, we want to solve the problem where if Player 1 had no card in the arena, Player 2's card showed up on Player 1's side. We need a player's cards to always show up on their own side.

Let's make a new branch called "cardPosition". To do that, you click on the branch name in the bottom left corner (see the red circle below) in VS code. That will pop up a menu to create a new branch or switch to a different branch:

Click on "+Create new branch…" and type cardPosition in the box that it shows you next and press Enter:

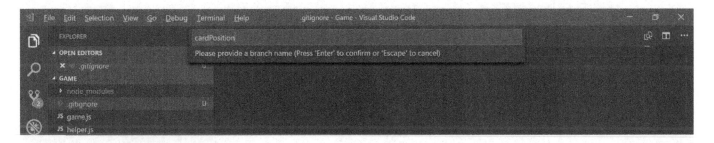

Now you will be on a branch called cardPosition.

Now let's solve the problem. One way to solve the problem is to make two `divs` inside the playerCards `divs` that are always there and then put the cards in those `divs`. Let's see the changes that were made using the differences in the code in VS Code. This is called a "diff":

The new `divs`:

Adding the cards to the new `divs`:

Look at the diff above. It says we removed those two lines and replaced them with two new lines. Now to update the styles:

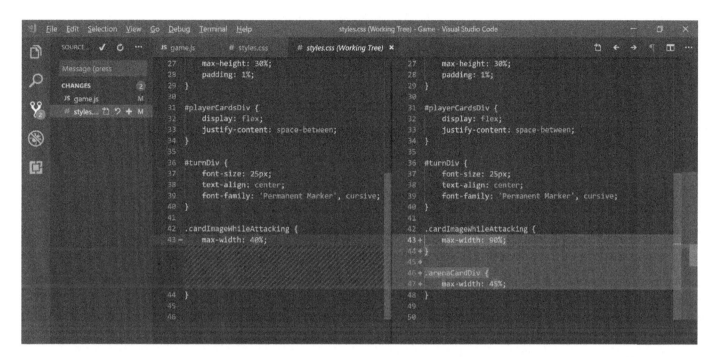

Let's see if our changes worked:

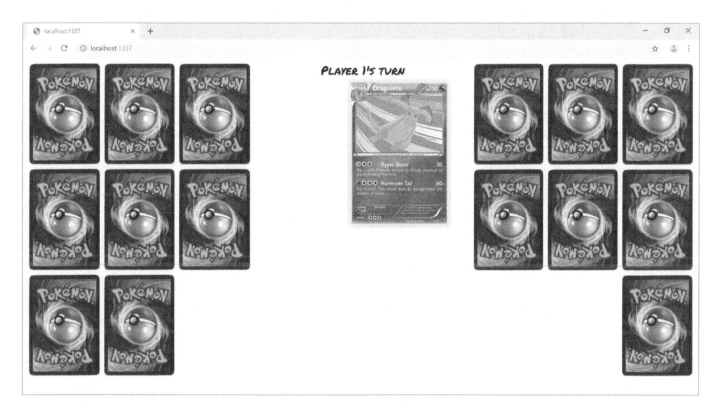

212

They did! Let's commit the code. Once we commit the code, we can't yet push it up to GitHub. We made this branch on our local computer. Before we can push this code up, we need to "publish" this branch first.

Press the little cloud button next to the branch name. That will publish the branch.

Merging and Pull Requests

Let's say you are managing this project and a friend wrote the fix for the card positions. Now you want to look at what changes they made to fix the card positions and then accept and merge all those changes into your game. There are many ways to do this. You can merge in VS code. But a really nice way to do this is with something called a Pull Request:

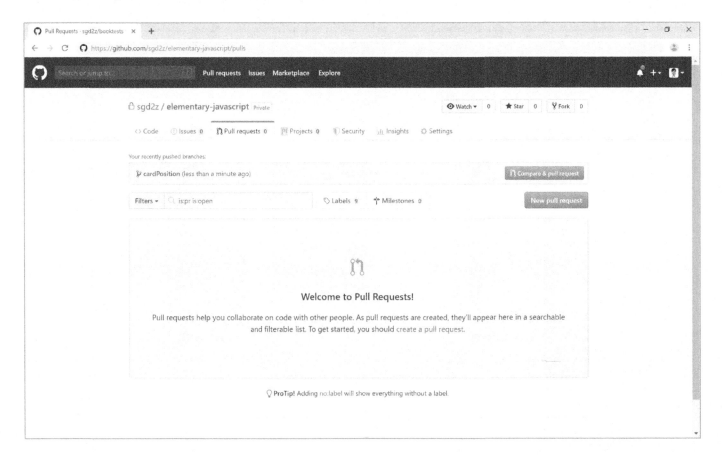

You can directly click on "Compare and pull request" or if that option is not available, click on "New Pull Request".

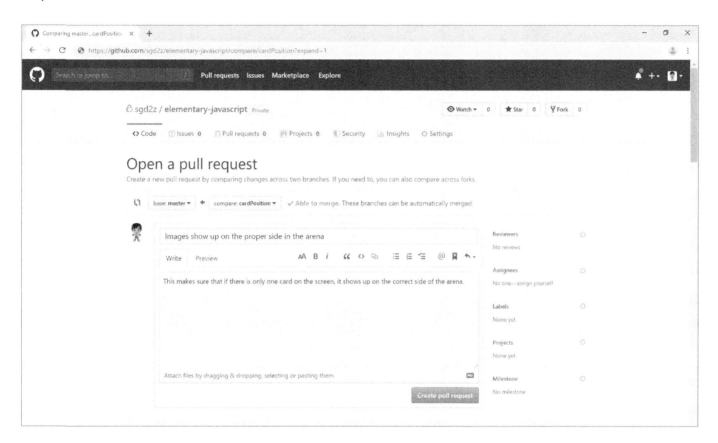

Select the branches and click "Create pull request". Once you do that, you will get to a page showing you the pull request:

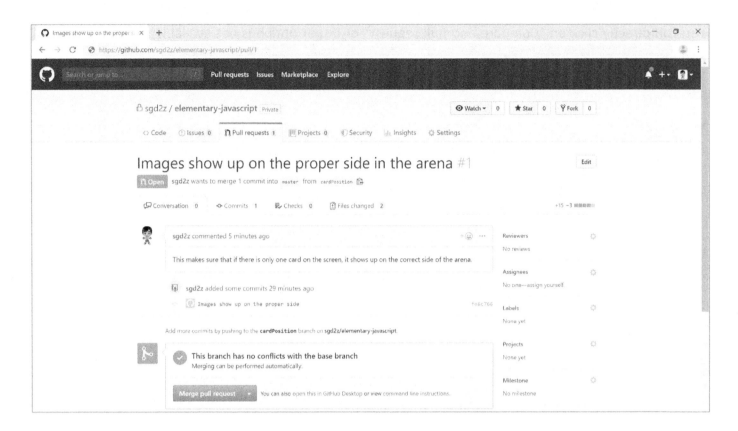

If you click on the "Files Changed" tab, you will be able to see the changes made:

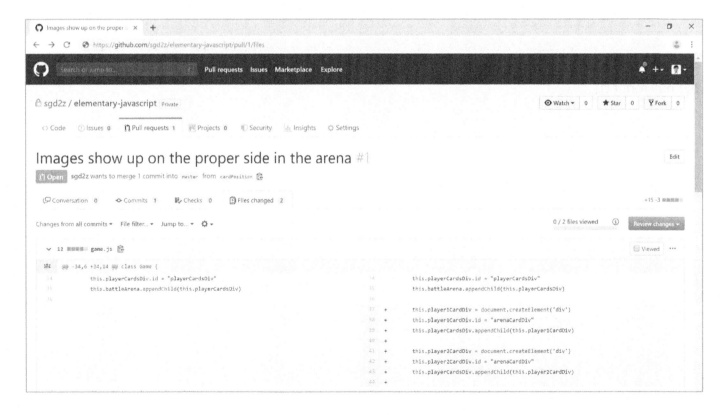

If you are ok with all the changes made, click on the "Conversation" tab and then click "Merge pull request" and then "Confirm Merge".

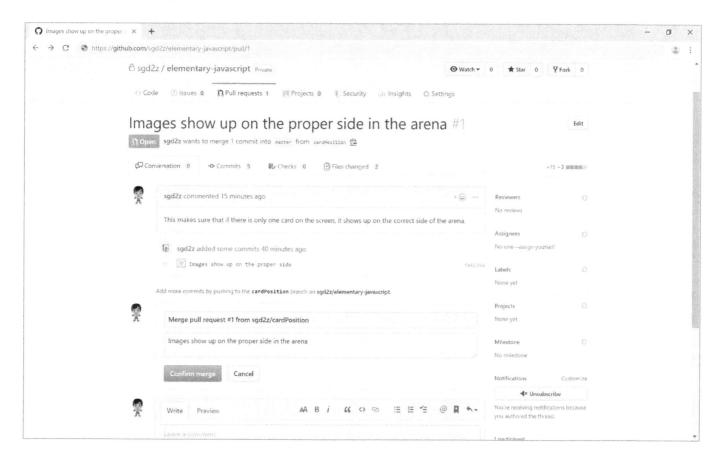

Once you click the "Confirm merge" button, all the code from cardPosition will be in the master branch.

Now we need to get all the changes that were made to master on our local copy of master. We can switch branches by clicking on the branch name at the bottom left. Switch to the master branch. Then we need to get all the changes by selecting pull from the same menu that we used to push:

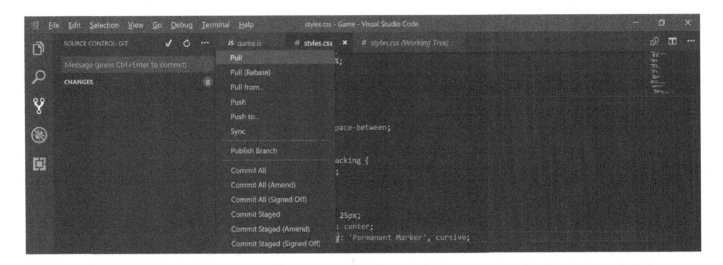

Now let's say while your friend was working on the cardPosition, you were trying to solve the error that sometimes causes the game to not load.

While you were still working on this, the cardPosition branch was merged into master. You should always make sure that what you are working on is updated with master.

On your machine, if you are working on the fixStartError branch, first commit (you don't need to push yet) all your changes. Then we need to merge master into our branch. For that, in VS Code, hit "Ctrl + Shift + P", like we did before for cloning and select merge:

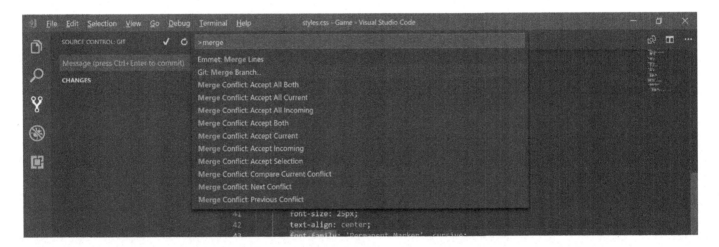

In the list of branches that show up, select master:

Once you do that all the changes from master will be merged into your branch. This way when you are making any fixes, you are always making them to the latest correct version of the branch.

Now that we have done that, let's go about fixing our error:

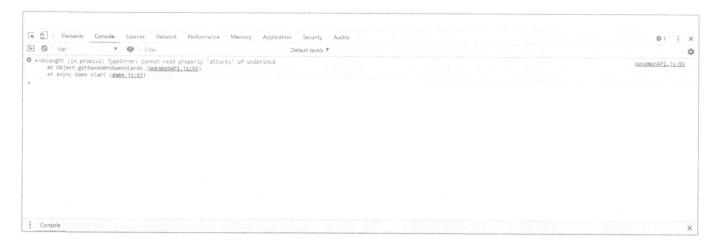

Clicking on the pokemonAPI.js:55 link, gets us to this point in the code:

It looks like sometimes we get to invalid Pokémon cards. Can you tell why that happens? How is it possible that the Pokémon card is not defined? Look at the line that selects the `randomIndex`. Do you see anything wrong with that? If looks like if we get an index of `pokemonList.length`, it will be beyond the list. Remember from the lists chapter, the last item in the list is list.length - 1. Let's fix that.

Sometimes we also get this error:

This one suggests that sometimes Pokémon don't have attacks. Let's fix that too. Before we commit, let's look at our changes:

```
/**
* Gets a random selection of Pokemon cards
* @param {Number} number the number of cards to get
*/
getRandomPokemonCards: async (number) => {
    // Get cards using the API
    let pokemonList = await PokemonAPI.getPokemonList()

    // Create a list
    let pokemonCards = []

    // Create a loop to get "number" cards
    let counter = 0
    while (counter < number) {
        // select a random card
        let randomIndex = randomBetween(0, pokemonList.length - 1)
        let pokemon = pokemonList[randomIndex]

        // create a new list of good attacks
        let goodAttacks = []

        // add all attacks where the damage can be converted to a number to good
attacks.

        let position = 0

        // if the pokemon has no attacks, move on to the next card
        if (pokemon.attacks === undefined) {
            continue
        }
        while (position < pokemon.attacks.length) {
            let attack = pokemon.attacks[position]
            attack.damage = parseInt(attack.damage)
            if (attack.damage > 0) {
                goodAttacks.push(attack)
            }
            position = position + 1
        }

        // replace attacks with good attacks
        pokemon.attacks = goodAttacks

        // only use pokemon that have good attacks
        if (pokemon.attacks.length > 0) {
```

```
            // create a PokemonCard object from the card to use in the game
            let pokemonCard = new PokemonCard(pokemon.name, pokemon.hp,
pokemon.imageUrl, pokemon.attacks)

            // add the card to our list
            pokemonCards.push(pokemonCard)

            counter = counter + 1
        }
    }

    console.log(pokemonCards)
    return pokemonCards
}
```

Now let's push this branch up and create the pull request. You can see the pull request here:

https://github.com/sgd2z/elementary-javascript/pull/2

Look at the code we added. It has something new in it that we haven't talked about in the book – continue – what does that do? Can you guess? That is a way in JavaScript to continue from the beginning of the loop without doing any code that comes after it. Basically, if the attacks are undefined, the program goes back to the beginning of the loop.

THE END AND A START

That's it. Now you know all you need to know to make a cool website or online game and many basics of writing code. I hope this is the start to some fun projects for you!

In the next book we will look at some more advanced things like how to make multiplayer games that you can play online with friends and maybe how to make games that have some two-dimensional graphics. If there are things that you want to learn, reach out to me.

If you have friends who also want to work with you on your game, pass this book onto them, make a repo, share it and get started!

If you do make something neat after reading this book, please email me and send me a link to your project! If there are parts of the book that are confusing or difficult to understand and follow, let me know. I will attempt to make them better in the next edition of this book. You can reach me at s1dd@s1dd.com. Put Elementary JavaScript in the subject of your email.

APPENDICES

APPENDIX 1

```javascript
const tableMaker = (number, upto) => {
    counter = 1
    while (counter < upto + 1) {
        document.write(number * counter)
        document.write('<br>')
        counter = counter + 1
    }
}

let n = 1
while (n < 11) {
    tableMaker(n, 20);
}
```

APPENDIX 2

```javascript
if (numberExistsInList(number, list) === false) {
    list.push(number)
}
```

APPENDIX 3

In *animal.js*:

```javascript
class Animal {
    constructor(name, type, color, weight) {
```

```
        this.name = name
        this.type = type
        this.color = color
        this.weight = weight
    }

    speak(whatToSay) {
        let div = document.createElement('div')
        div.innerHTML = this.name + ' said ' + whatToSay
        document.body.appendChild(div)
    }
    move(movementToMake) {
        let div = document.createElement('div')
        div.innerHTML = this.name + ' ' + movementToMake
        document.body.appendChild(div)
    }
}

export default Animal
```

In *iAmLearning.js*:

```
import Animal from './animal.js'

let lion1 = new Animal("simba", "lion", "orangishbrown", 500)
lion1.speak("roar")
lion1.move("run")

let horse1 = new Animal("horsey", "horse", "brown", 400)
horse1.speak("neigh")
horse1.move("trot")
horse1.move("gallop")
```

What that gets us:

```
simba said roar
simba run
horsey said neigh
horsey trot
horsey gallop
```

APPENDIX 4

```
/**
* Generates a random number between number1 and number2
* @param {Number} number1 an integer
* @param {Number} number2 an integer
*/
const randomBetween = (number1, number2) => {
    //calculate the range both numbers inclusive
    let range = number2 - number1 + 1
    // generate a random number in the range and shift it by number 1
    let randomNumber = Math.floor(Math.random() * range) + number1
    return randomNumber
}
```

APPENDIX 5

Countdown using `setTimeout`

```
// create a div to show the countdown
let countdownDiv = document.createElement('div')
document.body.appendChild(countdownDiv)

// Put the number of seconds to countdown in the div
let numberOfSecondsToCountdown = 10
countdownDiv.innerHTML = numberOfSecondsToCountdown

const countDown = () => {
    // decrease the countdown time
    numberOfSecondsToCountdown = numberOfSecondsToCountdown - 1

    // update the div with the number of seconds remaining
    countdownDiv.innerHTML = numberOfSecondsToCountdown

    // Stop counting when we reach zero
    if (numberOfSecondsToCountdown !== 0) {
        setTimeout(countDown, 1000)
    }
}
setTimeout(countDown, 1000) // Call the countdown function after a second
```